HANNIE RAYSON

Hannie Rayson is a graduate of Melbourne University and the Victorian College of the Arts (VCA) and has an Honorary Doctorate of Letters from La Trobe University. A co-founder of Theatreworks, she has served as Writer-in-Residence to the Mill Theatre, Playbox Theatre, La Trobe University, Monash University and VCA. Her theatre credits include *Please Return to Sender* (1980) and *Mary* (1981), each premiering at Theatreworks; and *Leave It Till Monday* (1984), which was first produced by the Mill Theatre. *Room to Move* (1985) won the Australian Writers' Guild AWGIE Award for Best Original Stage Play. Her next play, *Hotel Sorrento* (1990), a Playbox/Theatreworks co-production, also won an AWGIE Award as well as a NSW Premier's Literary Award and Green Room Award for Best Play of 1990. It has since had over fifty productions throughout Australia and overseas and has been translated into French, Japanese and Swedish. Her next two plays premiered at Playbox – *Falling from Grace* (1994), winning a NSW Premier's Literary Award, The Age Performing Arts Award, and touring to Japan in 1998; and *Competitive Tenderness* (1996). Hannie's television scripts include *Sloth* (ABC, Seven Deadly Sins) and co-writing two episodes of *Sea Change* (ABC/Artists Services). A feature film of *Hotel Sorrento*, produced in 1995, was nominated for ten Australian Film Institute Awards. In 1999 she received the Magazine Publishers' Society of Australia's Columnist of the Year Award for her regular contributions to HQ magazine.

D1342157

Other Titles in this Series

Hannie Rayson

LIFE AFTER GEORGE

NICK HERN BOOKS
London
www.nickhernbooks.co.uk

A Nick Hern Book

Life after George first published in Great Britain in 2002
as an original paperback by Nick Hern Books Limited,
14 Larden Road, London W3 7ST, by arrangement with
Currency Press Pty Ltd, PO Box 2287, Strawberry Hills,
NSW, 2012, Australia

Hannie Rayson has asserted her right to be identified as
the author of this work

Front cover design: Dewynters

Typeset by Country Setting, Kingsdown, Kent CT14 8ES
Printed and bound in Great Britain by Biddles of Guildford

A CIP catalogue record for this book is available from
the British Library

ISBN 185459 673 X

For my husband, Michael Cathcart
and my son, Jack Grant

Life After George received its British premiere on 30 January 2002 at the Yvonne Arnaud Theatre, Guildford, in association with Michael Codron and Lee Dean. It was produced at the Duchess Theatre, London, on 19 February 2002 by Michael Codron and Lee Dean in association with Mark Bentley and LHP Ltd. The cast was as follows:

PETER GEORGE	Stephen Dillane
BEATRIX GEORGE	Cheryl Campbell
LINDSAY GRAHAM	Joanne Pearce
ANA GEORGE	Susannah Wise
POPPY SANTINI	Anna Wilson-Jones
ALAN DUFFY	Richard Hope

Director Michael Blakemore
Designer Peter J Davison
Lighting Designer Paul Pyant
Music Kerry Davies
Sound Designers John Leonard and Robert Tory

Life After George was first performed on 1 January 2000
by Melbourne Theatre Company at The Fairfax, Victorian Arts
Centre, Melbourne. It was produced by MTC, and the cast was
as follows:

PETER GEORGE	Richard Piper
BEATRIX GEORGE	Julia Blake
LINDSAY GRAHAM	Sue Jones
ANA GEORGE	Asher Keddie
POPPY SANTINI	Mandy McElhinney
ALAN DUFFY	Rhys McConnochie

Director Kate Cherry
Designer Richard Roberts
Lighting Designer David Murray
Composer David Chesworth
Dramaturgs Hilary Glow and Michael Cathcart

Characters

PROFESSOR PETER GEORGE, *age 58 years.*

BEATRIX GEORGE, *the first wife, age 60 years.*

PROFESSOR LINDSAY GRAHAM, *the second wife, age 52 years.*

POPPY SANTINI, *the third wife, age 32 years.*

ANA GEORGE, *George and Beatrix's daughter, age 28 years.*

ALAN DUFFY, *George's best friend, age 59 years.*

Setting

The play is set in the present time, in the days leading up to the funeral of Peter George. The set needs to allow easy transitions from university, to funeral parlour, to pier, to various houses. The play also moves in and out of the 'memory zones' of the characters. These transitions rely on the fluid shifts of language and movement with a minimal use of stage machinery.

ACT ONE

ANA GEORGE *is playing Chopin on the piano. She is passionate – utterly abandoned to the music. The effect is magnificent.*

The lights fade to black. In the darkness we hear an ear-piercing scream. When the light comes up, ANA *is gone. We are in a University in Melbourne. A wild man in an academic gown flies onto the stage from the back of the auditorium. He flies above the audience's heads on a flying fox, gown billowing, bellowing with full voice. He lands on the top of the bench in the Public Lecture Theatre. He is* PROFESSOR PETER GEORGE.

GEORGE.
Oh I have slipped the surly bonds of earth,
And danced the sky on laughter's silvered wing,
And done a hundred things you have not dreamed of:
Wheeled and soared and swung – high in the sunlit silence.
I have plunged my craft through footless halls of air,
Reached out my hand
And touched the face of God.

Ladies and gentlemen. Welcome to the History of Revolutions. Welcome to the University. This is 1970 and it's your opportunity to take the joy-ride of your life.

We hear the sound of a plane flying low overhead, as though it is flying directly over the theatre. There is an almighty crash. The stage is plunged into darkness.

Funeral music. There is a coffin, centre stage. ALAN DUFFY *moves to the podium and addresses the audience.*

DUFFY. Ladies and gentlemen. Welcome. I'm Alan Duffy and I want to thank you all for coming today, to mourn the passing of our friend and colleague, Peter George. And to celebrate his remarkable life. In the thirty years I've known

George, I never met another man who could inspire people to engage with the world of ideas with such passion. Many of you are his students, some of you are his colleagues at the University. All of us are the beneficiaries of his intellectual legacy; his commitment to 'being an actor in the unfolding events of history'; his belief in the power of imagination; and his dedication to critical and rebellious thinking. Of his ten published works, it is the five-volume epic, *A History of the Australian People*, for which he will be best remembered. We are joined today by the three remarkable women in George's life. Beatrix George, his first wife.

Focus on BEATRIX.

Mother of his children, Ana and David.

Focus on LINDSAY.

Professor Lindsay Graham, George's second wife.

Focus on POPPY.

And the woman who has been at his side for the past two years. His third wife, Poppy Santini.

GEORGE *leaps off the bench in the Public Lecture Theatre, flourishing a text.*

GEORGE. 'The Idea of a University'. Cardinal Newman, 1852. A series of Discourses, delivered to the Catholics of Dublin over five successive Monday nights. To a room of, say, four hundred people – a room like this – Newman set out to define what a university might be and to defend the importance of a liberal education. Newman wanted us to cultivate a particular 'habit of mind' which he maintained would last through life. Its attributes: freedom, equitableness, calmness, moderation and wisdom. But what Newman omitted from his view of the liberal education – which is peculiar, given that Catholics by and large are very interested in this subject – is the imperative to engage in sex.

Let's face it, this is why you have come to university. Look around you. There are people here in this very room, with

whom you would like to have sex. Go on, look. More than
one, possibly two or three, perhaps at the same time. This,
in my view, is one of the primary goals of higher education.
To transcend fear and repression. Ladies and gentlemen, we
can only be fully human if we experience and reflect upon
the majesty of Eros.

We are the people of the seventies, the players in one of the
greatest revolutions in human history, forged, not by men at
war, but by men in love. The world of convention and
conformity, of collars and ties, twin-sets and pearls, and
brick veneers. This is the world that wants us to deny our
human potential. To clock on at 9 a.m.. To labour for the
profit of others. To do as we are told. To abandon our
human hunger for ideas and intimate, intelligent
engagement with the world in which we live.

If we are to become actors in the history of our times, we
must first claim back our minds and our bodies. We must
claim them from the power elites who want to own us. This
is what this moment in history has delivered up to us, ladies
and gentlemen. Unlike the people who have gone before us,
we are free to pursue sex for its own sake, as an end in
itself, without having to minister to something beyond, like
procreation. Your sexuality is the engine room of a
revolution.

Ladies and gentlemen, you are here for enlightenment. You
are here at the service, not just of your intellect, but of your
entire being. You have a choice. You can perform a series of
academic tasks and be rewarded with a degree. Or you can
commit yourself – mind and body – and live in the embrace
of the great universal questions. You are here to think
critically and rebelliously. To be magnificent and to fuck.
This is your moment in history. Seize it.

*He gathers his papers and leaves in a whirl. Lights come up
on* LINDSAY.

LINDSAY. I was there, that day. In the Public Lecture Theatre.
It was 1970. I thought he was the most inspiring man I'd
ever met. He had long, curly, black hair and a sort of
Sergeant Pepper jacket, tight jeans and elastic-sided boots

with Cuban heels. I thought – this guy is alternative to the core. I was twenty-one, editing the student newspaper, and going out with a boy I'd met at the Labour Club sherry party – Tom Parker. Tom burnt an effigy of the Vice-Chancellor and he was always inciting us to throw off our bourgeois values and unshackle our middle-class minds. As it happens I grew up in Flemington – my parents worked for the Post Office. We still had an outside loo – we weren't exactly middle-class. Not like Tom, whose family were card-carrying members of the Establishment. His main concern was that he didn't want anyone to know he'd been to Melbourne Grammar.

Anyway, I remember walking home after that lecture: I was so wired-up I forgot my bike. I left it chained up outside the Caf. There was so much to know and I wanted to know it all. Suddenly in the cosmology of my brain there was this galaxy of twinkling ideas, all of them tiny and unrelated, and they were floating in the vast black emptiness of my ignorance. The kind of knowledge that someone like George had, seemed unimaginably immense, like the Universe itself. It was all so exhilarating and yet so frustratingly out of reach. And then I had this brilliant idea.

She moves into the centre of the space. She knocks on the door of George's study.

Professor George? I was wondering whether you'd supervise my honours thesis?

GEORGE *closes the door of his study.*

(*To the audience.*) These days an academic would never close his door.

LINDSAY *enters the memory space of George's office. It is 1970.*

I want to write something about student radicalism . . . activism, beginning with Berkeley in 1964. I heard that you were in Paris in '68. During the May events at the Sorbonne? My sister told me you were part of the group that occupied the building, the liberated zone, wasn't it? And you were friends with Bertrand Russell, is that right?

GEORGE. Who's your sister?

LINDSAY. Janey Graham. Miss Freshette 1965.

GEORGE. Before my time.

LINDSAY. Of course. You were –

GEORGE. At Oxford. Go on.

LINDSAY. I haven't got anything really formulated, as such, but I want to show that there is a revolution going on. Even though people generally – out there in the real world – just think it's childish. (*Pause.*) My dad says the great weakness of student protest is that it's conducted by students.

She laughs.

GEORGE. And what do you think?

LINDSAY. Oh, I disagree. I have this friend. He's my –

GEORGE. Boyfriend?

LINDSAY. Yeah, in a loose sort of a way. He's more of a casual . . . er . . . friend. We're not really . . . well, we are – Anyway, Tom and I were talking to this guy in the pub about the importance of breaking the law, baiting police, challenging authority. That sort of thing. Anyway, this guy argued that student revolt is like a psychosis. Or something.

GEORGE. Yes. I've heard that argued. An Oedipal attack on social institutions which come to symbolise the hated father.

Pause.

LINDSAY. I think Freudian psychology stinks.

GEORGE *laughs.*

GEORGE. So you're going out with Tom Parker?

LINDSAY. Yes.

GEORGE. President of the SRC?

LINDSAY. Yes. Tom's got this thing about Che Guevara. He's obsessed with him actually. He's got posters everywhere – Che Guevara with Fidel in the hallway. Che moving among the Cuban people in his bedroom. Che playing chess, on the back of the toilet door.

GEORGE. Sartre said that Che Guevara was the most complete human being of our age.

LINDSAY. It seems to me that Che was only happy when he was in opposition. He got to be Minister of Education or Health or something in Cuba –

GEORGE. Industry.

LINDSAY. – Industry . . . and then he chucked it in to take up with this band of guerrillas in the Bolivian jungle. Tom thinks that's a glorious existential gesture, but I think it's the act of a man who's got a problem with aggression. I suppose you think I'm really bourgeois?

GEORGE. No. I think you're . . . marvellous.

LINDSAY. You do? See, I accept that we have to attack all the ruling structures, because the whole system is rotten to the core. But as I see it, the most radical act is to infiltrate the system from within. I'm not afraid of conflict.

GEORGE. That's good. Politics and conflict are rather inseparable twins, wouldn't you say?

LINDSAY. Tom says we have to think about ourselves being at war with the capitalist system because power and privilege corrupt.

GEORGE. Well, he'd know.

LINDSAY. What do you mean?

GEORGE. His family are the major shareholders in two of the biggest corporations in this country.

LINDSAY. I don't think he wants people to know that.

GEORGE. I'm sure he doesn't. I think we have to be careful we're not storming the presidential palace, merely to be seen smoking the old man's cigars. (*Pause.*) Tell me – Lindsay, is it? – what do you know about Karl Marx?

*

The Present. ANA *is back at the piano playing 'Something in the Air' by Thunderclap Newman.*

ANA. You can just see it, can't you, the old man seducing young girls while he's explaining the theory of surplus value? I'm Ana. George's daughter.

She sings the first few lines from 'Something in the Air.'

That was about as revolutionary as Ed Sullivan. You know, people say, 'It is so easy to be cynical about the sixties', but I think it's easier still to be romantic.

ANA *switches to 'Blowin' in the Wind'.*

I play a few bars of this and even the most apathetic baby boomer imagines that he or she was there at the barricades. Of course my father was there in Paris in 1968. He was there with my mother Beatrix.

Lights come up on BEATRIX.

BEATRIX (*to the audience*). When you tell people you were there in Paris during the events, this is greeted with amazement. It gave us a kind of credibility in Leftie circles – certainly in Australia – and George made the most of it. Naturally. If you run a course on the History of Revolutions and you were there when ten million workers went on strike, and it seemed as if everyone in Paris was taking to the streets, you could be excused for thinking it was one of the greatest movements of this century. There was a kind of delirium in the air. For a time there, they really believed they could bring down the de Gaulle Government. Mind you, no one had any idea of what they would actually do if that happened. But for George it was a defining moment. Being an actor, rather than a spectator, in history – that was his big thing.

BEATRIX *enters the memory space of her Paris apartment, 1968. She looks out her window, down to the street.*

We had a tiny apartment on the fourth floor. On Boulevard St Germain. We could just see Nôtre Dame from the bathroom window.

GEORGE *enters the apartment breathless.*

GEORGE. Bea, where were you? We were supposed to be meeting Daniel at the Deux Magots at five.

BEATRIX. I had some work to do. I'm sorry.

GEORGE. Guess who was there? Sitting at the next table? Simone de Beauvoir!

BEATRIX. Really?

GEORGE. I'm sure it was her. Reading Hegel and drinking hot chocolate. (*Pause.*) Oh God, I wish you'd been there at the Odéon this afternoon. I spoke for twenty minutes and you could have heard a pin drop. There were hundreds of people there, Bea, and they were hanging on every word. I was the best I've ever been.

He grabs her and kisses her neck.

(*In a mock French accent.*) The more I make the revolution, the more I want to make love.

BEATRIX *wriggles out from under him, good naturedly.*

BEATRIX. So what did you talk about?

GEORGE. I hadn't intended to speak, but I couldn't let this fellow get away with it. He was a Professor from the Sorbonne. A Gaullist, I suspect. He was incensed that so many of the teaching staff have joined the revolt. He was saying, 'They are civil servants and yet they're trying to overthrow the government which allows them all the liberties. This is just psycho drama! Verbal delirium.'

BEATRIX. I agree. It is.

GEORGE. It is not.

BEATRIX. Oh, for heaven's sake, George. Yesterday a man stood up and demanded the right to be able to urinate wherever he pleased.

GEORGE. Well, it's a democratic forum. The important thing is that everybody has the opportunity to –

GEORGE & BEATRIX (*together*). – express themselves.

GEORGE. What's the matter?

BEATRIX. Nothing.

GEORGE. There'll always be ratbags, Bea. You can't dismiss a revolution on the basis that one or two nutters jump on the bandwagon. That's the sort of argument your father'd come up with.

BEATRIX. It's all words. Just words. Don't you see? You can't build a future with words.

GEORGE. How else do you build a future? You have to start –

BEATRIX. But they're not interested in building things. All they want to do is smash things. When I ask, 'What sort of policies do you want to see introduced?', they haven't got a clue. They look at me with disdain that I should be so English and practical.

GEORGE. You can't create something new, if you can't imagine it. And that's what's happening, Bea. People are feeling free to imagine a new future.

BEATRIX. In my heart I know it's just an excuse for irresponsibility.

GEORGE. You can't see it, can you? Or you refuse to see it. Thirty thousand workers were in the street on Friday night. If you had bothered to come outside you would have seen it for yourself. These are men whose work in factories sentences them to a life of mind-numbing, body-mutilating enslavement to a machine that will render them cripples by the time they're fifty. They were seeing – glimpsing, for the first time – the possibility that with boldness and imagination they could just possibly defy their destinies. And life could be in some way different. But you grew up in Bowness-On-Windermere, in a very comfortable, very safe, very well-fed environment, and you know nothing about how other people live.

BEATRIX. And you grew up in Newcastle-Upon-Tyne, the son of a miner, which gives you working-class credentials which you will trade on for the rest of your life. Despite the fact that you have never done a day's physical work – Wait!

I came here to learn how to paint, George. I was accepted into the best art school in the world and it has been colonised by beatniks who don't want to make art. They want to make banal political slogans and force the rest of us to do the same. You came here to do your post-doctoral research which Professor Glen said was groundbreaking work. But you're not doing it. You haven't written a word for months. And for what? We're wasting our time, George. We may as well be home in England.

*

ANA. My father was writing a biography of Jean-Paul Marat. And Mum was a student of the École des Beaux Arts (the School of Fine Arts) – where the Atelier Populaire was established. You know the famous revolutionary posters?

*

In the Paris apartment, 1969. BEATRIX *is wrapping revolutionary posters in brown paper.*

BEATRIX. At least in England I can understand what people are talking about.

GEORGE. What are you doing?

BEATRIX. I'm sending these to Daddy.

GEORGE *is displeased.*

No one will know, George. Anyway, he's on our side.

GEORGE. How can he be on our side? He's a capitalist!

BEATRIX. He's very kind to the people at his factory. He even employs a black man. Mummy told me.

GEORGE. The revolution will not be over until the last capitalist has been hung by the entrails of the last bureaucrat.

BEATRIX. How can you say that?! He's my father.

GEORGE. How can you fail to understand? You cannot make sense of the system of oppression if you keep singling out individuals and saying, 'Oh, but he's not like that. He's not horrid.' You have to grasp this simple fact. Your father is a member of the ruling class.

BEATRIX *returns to address the audience in the present.*

BEATRIX. When my marriage to George was in its death throes, it came as a very deep shock to me that Lefties could be as indifferent to other people's suffering as any bull-necked capitalist. I found that profoundly disillusioning. I'm talking about how they treat people whom they purport to love. George's own mother is a case in point. Regardless of everything he believed about creating a more humane and just society, he left his own mother to die alone in a squalid hostel in Newcastle-Upon-Tyne. I suppose you think that's naive of me? To have imagined Lefties were exempt from indifference? But the terrible truth is – your average corporate warrior would have installed his mother in a comfortable pale pink room with soft blankets and fine tea cups. He might not have visited her because old people's homes made him feel nauseated – or mortal – but at least his mother would not be expected to fend for herself. While he was working – on his book about how the ruling class have taken away the dignity of the poor.

ANA. In 1969 they migrated to Australia. Mum hadn't finished at the Beaux Arts, but my father landed this job at the University here, as a lecturer in History.

The Paris apartment 1969.

GEORGE. You don't expect me to turn it down, do you, Bea? Of course I will, if it'll make you unhappy.

BEATRIX. I rang Daddy this morning and told him you'd accepted the job.

GEORGE. I haven't accepted. Yet. I'm not going, if you don't want to.

BEATRIX. Daddy said, 'Australian history? Good Lord. I didn't think they had any.'

GEORGE. They'll arrange everything. The woman said the house was very nice. Not dissimilar from the Latin Quarter. It's where the artists and intellectuals live, apparently.

BEATRIX. Whereabouts?

GEORGE (*shrugging*). Some place called . . . Box Hill.

*

POPPY. My mother used to be friendly with Arthur Boyd. When I was very young, six, maybe seven, she took me to Boyd's house and there on his easel was a painting of a beautiful woman stretched out in the long grass, naked. I remember standing there transfixed. The painting was still wet. And I thought, imagine being so beautiful that a man, an artist, would want to paint you. The woman was Beatrix. When George and I decided to get married you'd be surprised at the number of people who took me aside and said, 'He has been married twice before, you know'. Meaning, of course, that there must be something fundamentally untrustworthy about him. Frankly, I've had a string of boyfriends since I was fifteen. So what? Does that make me an emotional retard? Or does it just mean that it's taken me longer to find the right person? See – this is nothing against Beatrix or Lindsay, they're both perfectly nice women – but the truth is, they just weren't right. For George. It's so obvious to me. But sometimes you don't see these things yourself, do you, until it's too late.

POPPY *enters her memory.* GEORGE *is in the kitchen, cooking. He thrusts a pot at her.*

GEORGE. Taste that. Is that not the most exquisite boeuf bourguignon you have ever put in your mouth?

POPPY. That is beautiful.

GEORGE. You know the secret? Never use crappy wine in cooking.

POPPY (*referring to the label on the bottle*). Evans and Tate? George! You are the most extravagant man I have ever met. Is somebody coming for dinner?

GEORGE. Only my beautiful wife.

He grabs her. They kiss.

Hey, guess what? Random House rang me today. Some guy wants to write my biography.

POPPY. Wow. Who is it?

GEORGE. Never heard of him. Graham someone?

POPPY. What did you say?

GEORGE. I told him I was profoundly uninterested in my own life history.

POPPY. Oh, George.

GEORGE. On the two occasions I've been forced to rake over it, I've been in the divorce court. And I don't have great memories of either experience.

POPPY. It doesn't have to be that kind of biography. Does it? It should be about your work. Your ideas.

GEORGE. That's what I said. I said, 'If you're talking about a book of ideas, if that's what you're after, then let's begin.' Because we need to think hard about how we write about the sixties and the seventies –

POPPY. – without trivialising them.

GEORGE. That's right. And we need to do that because we need to understand what we've lost. We need to understand that, at the dawn of the new millennium, the most precious and profound human capacity is being spoiled. And smothered. And strangled. Do you know what I'm talking about? I'm talking about the human capacity for idealism.

*

BEATRIX. Two years ago. I went to see George, to say goodbye. That was when Raffaello and I moved to San Gimignano. In central Tuscany. Raffy's my husband.

George's study. GEORGE *appears climbing down a ladder with a book in his hand.* BEATRIX *enters her memory. It is 1998.*

I don't think you've done anything to the décor of this room for twenty years. You really don't have a very developed aesthetic, do you?

GEORGE. I used to have a wife who did all that for me.

BEATRIX. Raffy says that writers and academics are all the same. If you ever see an ad – 'Tuscan farmhouse, suit writer' – you know it means it's got no windows and the roof leaks.

GEORGE. How is Ruffy?

BEATRIX. Raffy. He's good.

GEORGE. Still invigorated by the sight of poverty in the street?

BEATRIX. You never let up, do you? Just because he works in the corporate world. Anyway, he's throwing it all in –

GEORGE. I have no doubt that Raffy is a very nice and cultured man. The fact that his business partner is Ron Williams is something I find harder to accept.

BEATRIX. You would be surprised. Ron is not what you think –

GEORGE. Oh, Beattie. You always think everyone is so nice and well-meaning. You refuse to accept that people are capable of wilful evil.

BEATRIX. People like Ron – they step out of their tower blocks in the city. They drive out to the leafy suburbs. And they don't see.

GEORGE. They see all right. Those bastards think this country used to be a namby-pamby sort of place. Run by wimpy liberal humanists who'd settle for the mediocre and the comfortable. But now there is real poverty on the street, they see it, Bea, and they feel energised by it. It serves as a real fillip. It says, 'Against all odds I've made it. I've competed and I've conquered. I am a winner. I'm in the winner's circle. I make winners.'

BEATRIX. You know, Ron Williams bought a piano for our daughter.

GEORGE. For Ana?

BEATRIX. She begged me not to tell you that.

GEORGE. Why would Ana accept a gift from someone like Ron Williams? Why would she do that?

BEATRIX. He offered. Maybe she's given up hope that her father would take an interest in her career.

GEORGE. Oh, Beatrix. That is low. That is really low.

BEATRIX. All I'm asking you to do is to look out for her occasionally. I know she's an adult and she can look after herself, but clearly she's not as self-possessed as some people her age.

GEORGE. You mean like Poppy? Is that what you're saying?

BEATRIX. I'm going to be ten thousand miles away, George. I'm hoping that you'll promise to be there for her.

GEORGE. Of course I'll be there for her. I always have been.

*

ANA (*to the audience*). I remember Dad coming home one night, when I was very young.

ANA *enters her memory. She is seven years old. It is 1979.*

GEORGE. Look at this, Ana. (*He holds up a football jumper.*) Do you know who wore this jumper?

ANA *shakes her head.*

A young bloke called Teddy Hopkins. They called him 'the mop-top rover'. He wore it in the 1970 Grand Final. I went to that match with Duffy, just two days before you were born. It was the greatest Grand Final ever. Carlton and Collingwood. Ted Hopkins was this kid from the sticks. Hardly had a game all year. Actually, when he was on the bench he had to wear glasses to see the play. Anyway, by half time the game was all over. Bloody Collingwood was thrashing us by six goals. We were just about ready to pack it in. Then Ron Barassi, the Carlton coach (and this is one of the decisions that made him a legend), Barassi says, 'Get ready, Teddy. You're on.' So this gawky, myopic boy runs out onto the MCG at the start of the third quarter. In the first two minutes he kicks two goals. You should have heard the crowd, Ana. This big red-faced woman in a blue beanie takes my face in her hands and kisses me smack on the lips. From that moment on we keep kicking goals. Teddy kicks another two, and the Blues come roaring back from the dead to win the flag! There we are in the outer, standing shoulder to shoulder with thousands of people. It was one of the great days of my life. It's one of the reasons I love this country. But do you think I can get that brother of yours to come with me? I was hoping you might.

ANA. Can I wear this?

GEORGE. You bet. And you know why you can wear it now?

He turns the jumper around and holds it up, showing the number on the back.

ANA. Because I'm seven.

ANA *returns to the present.*

(*To the audience.*) Every Saturday, we went to watch Carlton – Dad and I. My father really believed that all energy and ideas come from the people.

GEORGE. You have to understand that the people carry the weight of history on their backs.

ANA (*to the audience*). When you stood beside him in a footy crowd you felt part of a greater humanity. He made me feel this solidarity with the people around me. Anyway, when Mum took us away to England, I lost that feeling. I've always longed to get it back.

LINDSAY *flings open the door and storms into the kitchen of the Carlton house. It is 1993.* ANA *enters her memory zone.*

LINDSAY. How old are you, Ana?

ANA. Twenty-one.

LINDSAY. Twenty-one! Can you imagine a time, in the future, at any point in your life, that you will stop blaming your parents for who you are?

GEORGE. Lindsay. What's all this about?

LINDSAY. I'm fed up, George. I am sick to the back teeth of Ana wallowing in her own misery. (*To* ANA.) Your parents got divorced. I'm sorry. That's tough. Your mother took you away to England for three years. But your father has turned himself inside out to try make it up to you. And despite the fact that you have never, ever made any effort whatsoever to try to like me, I have worked incredibly hard to accommodate you in my life. And to help you. But what do I get? Nothing. You didn't even bother to show up.

She slams the door behind her. GEORGE *is bewildered.*

ANA. She found me a job as a typist in Administration at the University. (*Pause.*) What's the point?

*

GEORGE. My life has been about conversation. I have tried to keep the conversation going and if you want to write a history of that conversation then I'm with you, all the way. But if you want to run the metal detector over my psyche looking for tawdry explanations of my errant behaviour – then, I don't know, get yourself another corpse.

We hear the sound of a plane flying low overhead, as though it is swooping over the theatre and then flying off. The stage is plunged into darkness.

*

When the lights come up, LINDSAY *addresses the audience.*

LINDSAY. There I was, standing in the Museo Civico, in San Gimignano, one of the central hill towns in Tuscany. I'd been in Berlin when I heard the news. I can't remember anything much about that journey. I think I was in shock.

LINDSAY *enters her memory. High up on a ladder,*
working on restoring the ceiling frescoes, is BEATRIX.
The main room is lit by shafts of red and blue light from the
stained glass. LINDSAY *looks around her in awe. The*
room is sealed off from the public.

Bea?

BEATRIX. Up here! Good God! (*She makes her way down the*
ladder.) Lindsay! How did you find me?

LINDSAY. I asked the bus driver. He knew all about you. 'The
Australian – she works on the paintings in the Palazzo.'

BEATRIX. But how did you get in? We're closed for the
winter.

LINDSAY. An old man was in the courtyard. He had a key.

BEATRIX. Ah! That's Stephano.

LINDSAY. It cost me eight thousand lire.

BEATRIX. He makes a fortune with his keys. We call him Saint
Peter.

They embrace.

Well, welcome to San Gimignano. The city of beautiful
towers. And this is my corner of it.

LINDSAY. It's beautiful.

BEATRIX. It will be. Once upon a time it was a jewel box of
colour in here. Ruby red, cobalt blue, saffron gold. See the
parrots on the window wells? They were a deep green. And
on the ceiling there's dolphins.

LINDSAY (*looking around*). Those frescoes, they're almost
pagan, aren't they?

BEATRIX. They were painted in 1320. By Memmo di
Filippuccio. They're my favourite in the whole place.

LINDSAY. What are they? Wedding scenes?

BEATRIX. Some people say they were painted to warn men of
the deceitfulness of women. But I think they're rather more
jolly than that.

LINDSAY. Bea. George is dead.

BEATRIX. What? George?

LINDSAY. Ana hasn't – ?

BEATRIX. No. When? When did this – ?

LINDSAY. Yesterday. I got an e-mail. When I was in Berlin.

BEATRIX. An e-mail. Oh, how grotesque. How utterly grotesque. Oh, Lindsay. What happened?

LINDSAY. He crashed Duffy's plane on the Island.

BEATRIX. Oh, no.

LINDSAY. I don't know the details, Bea. But that's what happened.

BEATRIX. He crashed a plane. Oh, my God. Why would he do that?

LINDSAY. I don't know.

BEATRIX. Why would he do that?

LINDSAY*'s eyes smart with tears.*

Come on. Let's get out of here. (*She picks up Lindsay's case.*) We're not far. Just out of town. Raffaello's taken the car. He's in Sienna. You must be exhausted.

LINDSAY. I left Berlin at six this morning.

BEATRIX. Does Ana know?

LINDSAY. I don't know. I think so.

They exit. Lights come up on ANA *playing a hauntingly sad song.*

ANA. I haven't rung my mother yet. I can't bring myself to do it. I can't frame the words. I can hear her say, 'Ana, hello darling. What a surprise.' And then I'll have to say it. It's typical of this family. No one's ever here when you need them. David's my brother. He's gone AWOL in India. I had an address for him in Rajasthan, but he hasn't been there for two months. I assume he's all right. I couldn't think what to

do, so I left a message with the High Commission. I don't
imagine he'll want to come home. Why would he? If he
ever planned to sort things out with Dad, he's left his run
too late now. (*Pause.*) The last time I saw my father was
about ten days ago. We had dinner together for my birthday.
And on the sideboard there was this beautifully wrapped
present for me. It was a silver necklace. A rather extravagant
gift, I thought. It wasn't a particularly special birthday.
Anyway, Dad looked across with interest at the present.
It was obviously the first time he'd seen it. And when I read
the card it said, 'Happy birthday, Anna'. And my name was
spelt wrongly. I said, 'Dad, Ana's only got one "n". You've
spelt it with two.' He sort of shrugged and said, 'Oh that's
Poppy. She organised it.' I said, 'Don't you feel the need to
do anything?'

*

LINDSAY *comes down the stairs of Bea's Tuscan farmhouse.*
BEATRIX *is in the kitchen.*

LINDSAY. Was that a cow I just heard?

BEATRIX. It certainly was. We've got two. We're a two-cow
family.

LINDSAY. I can't believe you live like this. Growing olives
and bottling your own figs.

BEATRIX. Like an old peasant woman?

LINDSAY. Well, when you were living in Carlton I don't think
you even grew parsley, did you?

BEATRIX. This is ricotta, from the cows.

LINDSAY. Oh, my God.

BEATRIX. D'you think I've let myself go?

LINDSAY. I just can't believe you know how to do all this stuff.

BEATRIX. I don't. Paulo down the road makes the ricotta. But
it's from my cows. Here. (*Pouring some wine.*) Try some of
this: Vernaccia di San Gimignano.

LINDSAY. You didn't make it yourself, did you?

BEATRIX. No.

LINDSAY. Thank God for that. (*Pause.*) Cheers!

BEATRIX. Cheers! Here's to a happier occasion.

LINDSAY. You've really re-invented yourself, haven't you?

BEATRIX. So have you.

LINDSAY. No. I've just dug my heels in and stayed put.

BEATRIX. You're Dean of the Arts Faculty. I'd hardly call that 'staying put'. What were you doing in Berlin?

LINDSAY. Wheeling and dealing. As usual. Playing the corporate game. Trying to persuade the University of Berlin to send students to do postgraduate studies in Melbourne.

BEATRIX. Why would they want to do that?

LINDSAY. Well, precisely.

BEATRIX. Who would have thought it? You and I sitting by the fire in Tuscany, crying over our dead husband. (*Pause.*) I suppose we should contact whatsername.

LINDSAY. Poppy. You can't even bring yourself to say her name.

BEATRIX. Well, honestly . . .

   LINDSAY *laughs. Pause.*

LINDSAY. Will you come back with me for the funeral?

BEATRIX. Oh, I so badly don't want to do that. (*Pause.*) When are you going?

LINDSAY. I'm flying out of Rome tomorrow night.

BEATRIX. Oh, no. I couldn't possibly. Tomorrow. Good heavens. No. November is our busiest time. Because we're closed to the public. It's when we do the restoration work. Besides, Raffaello needs me here. We've got to finish picking. We're already late for the olive harvest this year. Some of the mills have already closed. I really don't think

I can get away. Besides, I hate funerals. I think they're morbid.

LINDSAY. But this is George.

BEATRIX. I know that. But funerals are for the living and I prefer to say goodbye in my own way. (*Pause.*) Anyway, I'm damn sure if it were my funeral, George wouldn't be trekking half-way across the world.

LINDSAY. I think at the very least he'd want to be there for his children.

BEATRIX. Oh, Lindsay, for heaven's sake. You've done this all your life and I think you should stop. This romanticising about George and his children. They've spent most of their lives without a father.

LINDSAY. That's just not true.

Silence.

BEATRIX. Anyway, it's too awkward. He's made a new life with that young woman and the day he married her was the day I said enough is enough. I said it – 'George, you are a ridiculous old fool and I am not going to spend another day of my life bothering about you'. And I haven't.

LINDSAY. I didn't realise you were so angry.

BEATRIX. Well. There you are. Neither did I.

LINDSAY. If it's a question of money . . . ?

BEATRIX. It's a question of dignity, actually. What are we supposed to do? Sit there with the girl's mother saying, 'Isn't it sad? She's been made a widow at thirty-two.' When actually she's in a very good position now to make a sensible choice and marry someone her own age.

LINDSAY. Yes. I'm sure she'll get over it.

Despite her best efforts, LINDSAY *cries. Long pause.*

BEATRIX. It's only humiliating if you allow it to be. After all, it was just vanity. The folly of a silly, old, middle-aged duffer.

LINDSAY. He made a mistake and he was very well aware of that.

Pause.

BEATRIX. Here, have some bruschetta.

*

POPPY *is standing on St Kilda Pier, looking south across the water to where the Island is. Near her on the pier is a lone fisherman, sitting on a stool. His face is obscured, but he is* GEORGE. POPPY *pays no attention to him. She talks out across the audience.*

POPPY. There is not a single person in the world who I can share this with. I can't be with anyone. I don't want to watch other people grieving. Because what they feel is nothing. There'll be so many of them circling, mingling, pushing sandwiches into their mouths, and spitting stories of how jolly funny it was when you said that or how frightfully shocked the Visiting Fellow was that day in the library and I don't want to hear it, George. Because it's all . . . inconsequential. Because there was only you and me. You spent a lifetime looking for me and then, there I was. And from that moment on we'd been together all our lives. And no one can ever possibly understand how profound that was. I didn't mind sharing you when you were alive. But I can't bear to share you now.

DUFFY *hurries along the pier. The fisherman,* GEORGE, *passes him on the pier.*

DUFFY. Poppy!

POPPY. Duffy.

DUFFY. Oh, my poor girl.

He embraces her.

I looked everywhere for you.

Pause.

POPPY. I didn't want to see anyone.

DUFFY. No.

POPPY. It was you who identified him?

DUFFY. Yes.

POPPY. I couldn't do that. I just –

DUFFY. Of course not.

POPPY. And could you . . . is he . . . ?

DUFFY. Yes. (*Pause.*) He's all right.

POPPY. He's not all right. He's dead.

DUFFY. Ssh. Ssh. I know. Ssh.

POPPY. I want to be with him. On my own. I don't want anyone else there. Do you understand me? I just couldn't go to the Coroner place, but I want to do everything else now. I don't know what it is you're supposed to do. This has never happened before, but someone will tell me, won't they?

DUFFY. I'll help you. I promise. I'll help you in every way I can. (*Pause.*) They'll transport him to the funeral place the day after tomorrow, so any time after that you can view.

POPPY. You're a doctor. I forgot. You've seen dead bodies before. You're used to it.

DUFFY (*fighting tears*). Yes. I'm used to it.

POPPY. Duffy. I want the funeral to be just us. No one else. You're his oldest and dearest friend . . . and I'm his wife.

DUFFY (*to the audience*). In the late seventies, George and I bought some land together on Flinders Island. It was a perfect arrangement. I had the plane – a 150-2 Cessna – but no cash. And George had the deposit for the land, but no way of getting there. Sometimes it was just George and me. We'd nick off for the weekend. Other times it'd be the whole lot of us – my wife Nell and our kids and George's kids and Beattie and then Lindsay. Poppy came once or twice, but I don't think she liked it much. Too much history. I'd been flying since I was a kid. My dad was a pilot. I remember the first time I took George up in the plane.

GEORGE *and* DUFFY *squeeze into the cockpit of the Cessna.*

I s'ppose we'd been in the air for about an hour.

DUFFY *is flying confidently. He steals a look at* GEORGE *who is white with fear.*

You all right?

GEORGE. Sure.

DUFFY (*yawning ostentatiously*). Aw, I'm a bit on the sleepy side. I might just take a nap.

GEORGE. What?

DUFFY. Take over will ya, mate?

GEORGE. Fuck off.

DUFFY *stretches out and tips his chair back.*

DUFFY. Got to learn some time.

GEORGE. Very funny, arsehole.

DUFFY. Whoops. Keep her straight and level. That's it. Keep the horizon about there on the windshield. Level with that dead insect.

GEORGE. Jesus, Duffy.

DUFFY. Pull back on the control column a bit. That's it. Push it in and you're gonna see a lot of ground.

GEORGE. Duffee!

DUFFY. See that gadget there, that tells you how high you are. We're cruising on about two and a half thousand feet. If you wanna take a closer look at something, push down. Nice and slow. Insect falling. Falling. A thousand feet, you'll see cars. Five hundred feet, you'll see sheep. But once you start to see their legs, you know you're in trouble. You right now? Keep the sky level. That's the main thing. Wake us in about half an hour.

GEORGE *vomits.*

Oh, mate . . .

GEORGE (*pathetically*). Just drive the plane, arsehole.

DUFFY *re-enters the present. He addresses the audience.*

DUFFY. He was coming in to land, like he'd done a hundred
times before. He must have encountered a wind shear.
It was a freak thing. Wind coming at you from different
directions. At different levels. He lost control. He didn't
have the air speed. He crashed at the end of the runway.

DUFFY *enters his memory. He is reading the* Herald.
GEORGE *is flying confidently.*

GEORGE. I thought I might take her out for a spin next
Thursday. That all right with you?

DUFFY. I play golf on Thursdays.

GEORGE. I know.

Pause.

DUFFY. Sure.

Pause.

GEORGE. I've got a post-grad student who's never been in a
plane. Can you believe it?

DUFFY *doesn't say anything.*

I think this student is probably the most original thinker I've
ever had.

DUFFY. What's his name?

GEORGE. It's a woman.

DUFFY *looks across as if to say, 'Derr'.*

Her name's Poppy. (*Pause.*) No, I promise you. This girl is
amazing. She is writing her thesis on what she calls 'social
nostalgia'. Basically she's critiquing people like us for our
nostalgia for the seventies. It's about the demonisation of
youth by the baby-boomer generation.

DUFFY. Is she beautiful? (*Pause.*) George?

GEORGE. Everything you could want. (*Pause.*) Duffy?

DUFFY. Hmm?

GEORGE. Would you say I was a competitive sort of person?

DUFFY. Not particularly.

GEORGE. Ambitious?

DUFFY. Reasonably. (*Pause.*) Why?

GEORGE. I feel as though Lindsay competes with me. Every day. About even the smallest thing. She has a bigger office than I do, in the Faculty Building. She has more Honours students asking her to supervise their theses. She can write faster. She publishes more. In fact she is superior in every way, really. For instance, last night I spent six dollars on two A4 batteries, when apparently you can get them at Coles for four dollars ninety-nine.

DUFFY. Aren't you a fucking idiot?

GEORGE. It's exhausting.

DUFFY. How's that business with the reflux, the acid in your stomach? I forgot to ask you last week?

GEORGE. Gone. It's just tension.

DUFFY. Good. (*Pause.*) Maybe you should talk to Lindsay about this competitive stuff.

GEORGE. She's too busy, mate. Climbing up the career ladder. In fact she's dancing on the glass ceiling at the moment.

*

POPPY. Duffy?

DUFFY. Sorry?

POPPY. Did you hear what I said?

DUFFY. Sorry. I was a million miles away.

POPPY. I want the funeral just to be for us.

DUFFY. I know. I heard you. (*Pause.*) I don't think that's going to be possible. For a start, there's Ana. She has the right to mourn the death of her father.

POPPY *enters her memory zone. It is 1995. She is walking through the campus with* GEORGE. ANA *intercepts them by surprise. It is as though she has been waiting for them.*

ANA. Dad!

GEORGE. Ana. Gosh. What are you doing up here?

ANA. I thought you might like to take me out to lunch. Hello.

GEORGE. Poppy. This is my daughter Ana. Poppy Santini.

POPPY. Hi.

GEORGE. Look, I just can't, sweetheart. I wish you'd rung. I've got a meeting . . .

ANA. Right.

POPPY. George, I'm really happy to do this another – (*time*)

GEORGE. No. I really need to discuss that . . . chapter . . . with you.

ANA. Is he supervising you?

POPPY. Yes. (*Pause.*) He's the best.

ANA. Well, that's what you want, isn't it? The best. (*Pause.*) You don't look like a university student.

POPPY. I work part-time. For a publisher.

ANA. I was having a wander around the Student Union. There's this lecture at lunchtime: 'Can Capitalism Survive?' (*Beat.*) God, university students are gits.

POPPY *and* GEORGE *laugh nervously.*

I've always thought university students were major dickheads. That's why I never wanted to come here. Especially the women. Imagine having an affair with your lecturer? Really.

GEORGE. Ana –

ANA. You know, people our age who think feminism is just a crock of shit, do tend to become victims in the same way our mother's generation did. Don't you think?

*

LINDSAY (*to the audience*). On the flight home from Rome I told the boy sitting next to me that I was going home to bury my husband. It turned out that he was one of our students and he'd taken George's subject – the History of Revolutions. Apparently George had given this kid a mark of 101 for his final essay. He was a sweet boy. Very sympathetic. And sensitive. He said, 'What do you do?', and I told him I was the Dean of Arts. He looked really perplexed. He said there was a rumour going around that the Dean was trying to shaft Professor George, but that couldn't be true, could it? You'd hardly shaft your own husband. But by then I was in too deep. I couldn't say, I'm not actually married to him anymore.

LINDSAY *enters her memory space. George's study 1970.*

I've just been reading Engels.

GEORGE. Well done.

LINDSAY. It's so radical. So now . . . did you know that the original meaning of the word 'family' is domestic slave? *'Famulus'*. This is in Roman times. And *'familia'* is the total number of slaves belonging to one man. That's the origin of the family – slavery. I'm never going to get married.

GEORGE. So you're suggesting that Engels was a Women's Libber?

LINDSAY. Yes. He was. He saw that marriage was a kind of microcosm of society. The husband is the bourgeois and the wife, the proletarian. Which is exactly how it is. The modern family is founded on the slavery of the wife.

GEORGE. Of course the Marxist would argue that class is the dominant concept. It's in the alienation of the worker – male and female from the means of production – that we see essential slavery.

LINDSAY. But Engels –

GEORGE. See, you can't escape one fundamental fact. The wife, the mother, through her body, creates life. The male worker is selling his body. He is a tool of capitalism. He is giving his life away.

LINDSAY. But women are selling themselves once and for all to the service of a husband.

GEORGE. I suspect you may have a rather jaundiced view of marriage. In my experience women tend to like it. But listen to me. I think you're getting side-tracked. I am fully aware that the subjugation of women is very in at the moment. But don't be swayed by intellectual fashion. There are profound questions, Lindsay, that people like you should be addressing, like the ownership of wealth, who is exercising power in this country. Why there is evil in the world.

LINDSAY. Sometimes it's so confusing talking to you. I read and I talk to other people and I get things all worked out and then I talk to you and you blow it all away.

GEORGE. I'm sorry. I don't mean to do that.

LINDSAY. I thought if I quoted from Engels you'd be more persuaded?

GEORGE. I don't need persuading –

LINDSAY. Rather than Mary Wollstonecraft or Susan B. Anthony or Emma – (*Goldman*)

GEORGE. Look, I totally accept the principle of equality between the sexes. I remember reading an essay by John Stuart Mill. This was years ago – when I was at Oxford – and he affirmed what I had always believed. The subordination of one sex to another is wrong and one of the chief hindrances to human improvement.

LINDSAY. One of the women in my reading group said you were a chauvinist. I knew she was wrong.

Pause.

GEORGE. Well, I've always held her in high regard too.

LINDSAY (*shocked*). Do you know who I'm talking about?

GEORGE (*laughing*). No.

LINDSAY. I can't understand how any woman would surrender her future just to become somebody's wife. A man's sexual property.

She walks over to the window.

GEORGE. And why would someone brilliant and beautiful like you, have to surrender to anyone?

Beat.

LINDSAY. I want to be free to have sex with whomever I choose.

GEORGE. Presumably with whomever's consent.

LINDSAY. You're making fun of me.

GEORGE. No, I'm not.

LINDSAY *picks up a framed photo of* GEORGE *and* BEATRIX.

LINDSAY. Is this your wife?

GEORGE. Yes.

LINDSAY. What's her name?

GEORGE. Beatrix.

Pause.

LINDSAY. I've been thinking . . . if people must get married they should have open marriages. Monogamy's unnatural. Everyone knows the most intense form of sex is infidelity. (*Pause.*) Engels says that probably the only reason the Catholic Church abolished divorce was because it had convinced itself that there is no more a cure for adultery than there is for death.

GEORGE (*laughing*). You really are something.

They embrace for the first time.

LINDSAY. I've always thought it was impossible for a conservative to be good in bed.

They kiss.

GEORGE. Now there's a subject for a book.

They kiss.

LINDSAY. You'd have to do the research.

GEORGE. Sleep with people in the Liberal Party.

LINDSAY. I'd rather kill myself.

They kiss.

*

Duffy's house. The present. DUFFY *puts a blanket over* POPPY *lying on the couch. There is a knock at the door.*

DUFFY. Lindsay!

LINDSAY. I hope this is all right.

She is carrying her luggage. They embrace.

DUFFY. You moving in?

LINDSAY. No. I've just come straight from the airport. I am totally emotionally wrung out. How are you? Actually, Duffy, could I use your bathroom?

DUFFY. 'Course.

LINDSAY. Thank you. And I would kill for a cup of tea.

LINDSAY *exits.*

DUFFY (*to the audience*). Lindsay. Just the same.

DUFFY *enters his memory space. It is 1972.* GEORGE *and he are having a beer at a Carlton pub.*

GEORGE. What do you make of all this women's rights business?

DUFFY (*chuckling*). Just keep your head down and wait till it blows over, I reckon.

GEORGE. I can see the validity in it.

DUFFY. Yeah. So can I.

GEORGE. But it's a bit like taking the dog for a walk on a lead. You can see the benefits but, jeez, it's a drag.

*

LINDSAY *appears carrying a very large diary.* DUFFY *is in the kitchen, but within talking range.*

LINDSAY. I've drawn up a list of absolutely everything I can think of. Funeral notices, floral tributes, cars, civil celebrant – I've got a suggestion, by the way. I assume you've chosen an undertaker? I thought Tobin Brothers. They were marvellous when Mum died.

DUFFY *arrives with a cup of tea.*

Lovely. Thank you. I don't know what it is with airline catering. You wouldn't think it could be that hard to provide a decent cup of tea.

DUFFY. It's the milk.

LINDSAY. Oh, right. The person I was thinking of – did you go to Marshall Robertson's funeral?

DUFFY. No.

LINDSAY. Oh, she was marvellous, Duffy. Truly. The celebrant. George thought so too. There was plenty of space for the family to be involved with readings and poetry. That sort of thing. But the celebrant spoke so eloquently and rather profoundly, I thought. And personally I'd be more comfortable if we had a woman –

DUFFY. Lindsay! (*Pause.*) Slow down.

LINDSAY. There's such a lot to organise. And I just knew I'd have to hit the ground running. Ah! Patricia Browne! She'll know who that celebrant is. Have you got a biro, Duff? I think I must have left mine in the seat pocket. I'll ring Patricia Browne, first thing.

DUFFY. Lindsay. Poppy is very fragile. At the moment. She doesn't really know what kind of funeral she wants, yet.

LINDSAY. No. Well . . . (*Pause.*) Beatrix is coming. By the way. She should be getting in tomorrow afternoon. I had to pull some strings to get her on a flight at such short notice.

DUFFY. Bea's coming?

LINDSAY. Yes. They're always so booked out. Anyway, tell me, how's Ana? She's the one I'm really worried about.

DUFFY. I think she's all right.

POPPY *wakes up. She is still groggy from the effects of a sleeping tablet. Both women are taken aback to see each other.*

POPPY. Lindsay!

LINDSAY. Oh. Poppy.

POPPY. I thought you were in Europe.

LINDSAY. I was. Yesterday. Or the day before. Whenever it was. You lose track, don't you, when you get back? That's been my experience. It takes at least two or three days. Mind you, I don't feel the effects the other way around. I just jump straight off the plane. I don't know why that is. How are you? Terrible, stupid question.

POPPY. I'm completely out of it, actually. What was that you gave me, Duff? A horse tranquilliser?

DUFFY. Just a sleeping tablet. Here. Sit down. Would you like some tea?

POPPY. No, I'm fine. Thank you. (*Noticing Lindsay's suitcases.*) You've come straight from the airport?

LINDSAY. Yes. I thought you might need –

POPPY. That was very kind of you. How did you know I was here?

LINDSAY. Oh, I don't know. I just thought –

POPPY. Kind, lovely Duffy. What would we do without you? (*To* LINDSAY.) I'm touched that you came. George always said you were marvellous in a crisis. (*Pause.*) I've been wandering about on my own. Duffy found me down on the pier. What day is it?

DUFFY. Tuesday.

POPPY. Tuesday. I haven't been home since Saturday. Even though every part of me wants to be alone, I can see it's not a good idea. I think I probably came very close to throwing myself in the sea.

LINDSAY. Mmm.

DUFFY. Not a good idea.

LINDSAY. No. It's probably a bit cold.

Beat.

POPPY. When you love someone as much as I loved George, perhaps you could be forgiven for being a bit irrational.

Pause.

DUFFY. Lindsay had an idea for a celebrant.

POPPY. I don't want a celebrant. Sorry. But I don't. I don't want some strange person eulogising my husband when he or she didn't even know him.

LINDSAY. This woman was very good. I was terribly –

POPPY. No. No Church. No religious gumpf. No strangers. (*Pause.*) I was hoping you'd do it, Duffy.

DUFFY. Oh.

LINDSAY. With respect, that person needs to be a good public speaker. Not that –

POPPY. Duffy's great. Haven't you ever heard him? Oh, you weren't at our wedding, were you?

LINDSAY. No.

POPPY. You were invited.

LINDSAY. I know.

POPPY. Please, Duffy. It's what George would have wanted. It's just whether you feel you'd be up to it.

DUFFY. Without breaking down.

POPPY. I wouldn't mind.

LINDSAY. Oh no, I don't think . . . The reason I was suggesting the celebrant is because in a public event like this, I think we'd all feel more secure if the occasion were being managed by a professional. Or at least someone . . . one step removed. (*To* DUFFY.) I think you'd probably feel more comfortable too. (*To* POPPY.) Funerals can be enormously stressful occasions. I don't know how much experience you've had.

DUFFY. I'd like to do it actually. I think Poppy's right. George'd prefer it.

POPPY *hugs him. In the moment, they both start to cry.* LINDSAY *waits.*

POPPY. Sorry.

LINDSAY. Personally, I think we should put off all decisions until tomorrow. When we've all had some sleep, and we can involve Ana, and of course Beatrix will be back by then.

POPPY. Beatrix?

LINDSAY. Yes. She's coming back for the funeral.

Pause.

POPPY. I was hoping it'd be just a small affair.

LINDSAY. Mmm. Poppy, it might have been different if George was . . . like my mother, for example. We had a very small family funeral. Just a few people. But I think you might have to accept that he was a very well-known and highly-regarded public figure. And there will be people from the University, the media, the Labor Party, who will want to pay their respects. I expect there could be anywhere up to four hundred people there. And there will be talk of some sort of public memorial. A statue maybe or a fountain. I don't know. There'll certainly be a Festschrift.

POPPY. A what?

LINDSAY. Festschrift? It's an academic thing. People get together and talk about the influence of the person's scholarship on their own work and then they publish the papers.

POPPY. Oh.

LINDSAY. That's what I was saying. There's a lot of
organising. So, let me just clarify one thing. Have you made
a time to meet with the funeral arranger?

DUFFY. Tomorrow afternoon, I think.

LINDSAY. Mmm. Let's make it Thursday morning. I've got a
Faculty Board meeting then, but I'll cancel it. That way Bea
can be involved, and one of us can contact Ana. Do you
want to do that, Duffy, or will I? Look, I will. I want to
speak to her anyway. There isn't any rush with these things,
you know. People assume you've got to hurry up and get
the funeral over and done with. But there's no time limit.
Legally speaking. We can take as long as we like.

*

Lights come up on a smoky late-night cabaret club where ANA
is playing the piano. This is a regular gig. It is 1 a.m. and
ANA *is just finishing her final bracket when* BEATRIX *walks
in and finds a seat. She sips a drink watching her daughter
play. As* ANA *packs up* BEATRIX *approaches.*

ANA. Mum.

They embrace.

What are you doing here? It's 1 a.m.. I thought you would
have been dead to the world.

BEATRIX. That motel is on a freeway. I can't sleep.

ANA. You should've taken a tablet.

BEATRIX *casts a scrutinising eye over* ANA'*s outfit.*

BEATRIX. You could try a bit harder, don't you think?

ANA. No.

BEATRIX. Those pants look like they're held together with
sticky tape.

ANA. Staples actually.

BEATRIX. Oh, Ana!

ANA. As if anyone would notice. It's dark in here.

BEATRIX. I noticed.

ANA. Yes, but you're my mother. And you're not typical of our regular clientele.

BEATRIX. What is your regular clientele?

ANA. Losers mostly.

BEATRIX. Oh, Ana.

ANA. Oh, Mum. (*Pause.*) Lindsay rang me today – in Chief Executive mode. She's got plans for the funeral. It's like she's working for Melbourne Major Events.

BEATRIX. You could've predicted that, couldn't you?

ANA. She'll be seeking corporate sponsorship soon. Why does she do this?

BEATRIX. I was thinking about this on the plane. If I wasn't here, it'd be just her and Poppy and that would make Lindsay the ex-wife. But now I'm here, she can garner more status as being the main wife. And then she can run everything. Do you think that's uncharitable?

ANA (*laughing*). It's so entirely plausible, it's hilarious.

BEATRIX. I really don't like her.

ANA. You don't say!

BEATRIX. I'm nice to her. But I don't mean it. (*Pause.*) Actually I felt a bit sorry for her in San Gim. She looked so lost.

ANA. Why did you come then?

BEATRIX. I wanted to be here for you.

ANA. That's nice of you.

BEATRIX. I'm your mother.

ANA. I feel as though I've been hoisted up the genealogical ladder a notch. Sort of prematurely. Did that happen to you when your father died?

BEATRIX. I don't know. I certainly feel like that now. Ana, you have got holes under the arm of that shirt. Honestly. Let us go tomorrow and buy you some proper clothes.

ANA. Mum. I am twenty-eight.

BEATRIX. I know. It's a disgrace. (*Pause.*) Anyway, are you all right? In yourself? Are you eating properly?

Pause.

ANA. Are you referring to my weight?

BEATRIX. I don't mean to be . . . personal.

ANA. Oh, Mum. You are always personal.

BEATRIX. Well, you do seem to have filled out a bit.

ANA. Can you quit this please?

BEATRIX. Okay. (*Pause.*) Often it's a sign of being unhappy. That's all.

ANA. I really don't want to have this conversation. (*Pause.*) And I am unhappy. You're right. My father died on Saturday.

BEATRIX. Mmm. I know. But you haven't put on that much weight since Saturday.

ANA. Let's go!

BEATRIX. No. Let's not. I'm sorry. I won't say another thing. I'm just concerned.

ANA. You are not just concerned, mother. You are judgmental. Because I don't look like Sally-Ann Morell-Foster. 'Even though I had all the same opportunities.'

BEATRIX. I don't want you to look like Sally-Ann Morell-Foster. Although she's very attractive and she married well. (*Beat.*) Just a little joke.

ANA. It's not funny. It's oppressive. (*Pause.*) You know, for all the crap that you and Dad go on with about being libertarian, you actually wish I was a more conventional person. If you were honest you'd say you were disappointed.

BEATRIX. All I want is for you to be happy.

ANA. You want me to be married to a handsome lawyer called Jason and live in Hawthorn.

BEATRIX. Why don't you come back to San Gim with me, for a few months?

ANA. I want you to tell me the truth.

BEATRIX. Okay. The truth is, the only person who can't accept you, Ana, is you.

*

The funeral parlour. LINDSAY is waiting in the reception area. POPPY arrives wearing dark glasses.

LINDSAY. How are you this morning?

POPPY nods, unable to speak.

Could I get you some water?

POPPY nods. LINDSAY enters her memory zone. It is 1989. GEORGE is sitting at the kitchen table nursing a hangover.

Here. Have some water. Perhaps you're too old to be out drinking and flirting with young girls.

GEORGE. Don't be vulgar, please. I note that you didn't come in at all, the night before last.

LINDSAY kisses his forehead.

LINDSAY. The difference is, I don't fall in love with them.

GEORGE. You know what I hate about this set-up? The fact that we have to respect each other's privacy.

LINDSAY. I don't want to know the details.

GEORGE. There are no details, Lin. You're the one who's got secrets. (*Pause.*) There is no point in having a marriage if there are secrets? Is there?

LINDSAY. We're very compatible, domestically.

GEORGE. How ghastly.

LINDSAY. Passion isn't everything, George.

GEORGE. Yes it is. For me, it is.

*

LINDSAY *returns to the couch and hands* POPPY *the glass of water.*

LINDSAY. Can I ask you something? George told me once that you and he had sex every day. Is that true?

POPPY. Yes.

Long pause.

LINDSAY. I don't suppose I really needed to know that, did I?

BEATRIX *arrives, also wearing glasses.*

BEATRIX. Sorry I'm late. Hello, Poppy.

POPPY. Hi.

They embrace, tentatively.

LINDSAY. No Ana?

BEATRIX. No. And Duffy? Is he coming?

POPPY. He'll be here shortly. He plays golf on Thursday mornings.

BEATRIX. Gosh, that's right.

LINDSAY. A creature of habit, our Duffy.

POPPY. Yes.

BEATRIX. Poppy, I don't feel completely comfortable being here. If you would rather make these arrangements on your own –

LINDSAY. Bea. You and George were together for fourteen years. You're the mother of his children. You've got more right to be here than either of us, really. It's five past. Perhaps we won't wait for Duffy. I should tell them we're ready.

BEATRIX *enters her memory zone. It is 1976. She is in her kitchen. There is a knock at the door.*

BEATRIX. Come in. It's open.

LINDSAY *appears.*

LINDSAY. Beatrix?

BEATRIX. Yes.

LINDSAY. I'm Lindsay Graham.

BEATRIX. Oh. Hello. George isn't here at the moment. He's at the University.

LINDSAY. I know. I've come to see you.

BEATRIX. Me?

LINDSAY. Yes. (*Pause.*) I'm a feminist. And as such I feel my first loyalty is to my sisters.

BEATRIX. Your sisters?

LINDSAY. Other women. (*Pause.*) I believe in taking responsibility for my own actions. If we want to have equality, we also have to take responsibility. We can't just leave things up to men –

BEATRIX. No?

LINDSAY. So I thought I should come and see you. And tell you myself. I'm having an affair with George.

BEATRIX *is speechless.* BEATRIX *and* LINDSAY *return to the couch.*

POPPY. Have you had any luck finding David?

BEATRIX. Sorry?

POPPY. Your son?

BEATRIX. Oh, David. He's in India.

POPPY. Yes.

BEATRIX. They said he was going to be back in the village, today or tomorrow. So, hopefully, I can speak to him then.

POPPY. That's good.

BEATRIX. I really don't think he'll come back for the funeral. I'm not going to push it. I don't know whether that's the right thing or not.

LINDSAY. My sister didn't go to Mum's funeral. She says she's always regretted it. No sense of closure.

BEATRIX. Well, it's up to him. He's a grown man.

POPPY. I just want to give him the option.

BEATRIX. Yes. (*She looks at* POPPY.) Thank you.

LINDSAY. I do think we should fix the date today. If nothing else.

BEATRIX *and* POPPY *exchange a glance. As* LINDSAY *gets up to look for a staff member,* POPPY *watches her.* POPPY *enters her memory zone. Lindsay's office, 1996.*

POPPY. I just want you to know that I have a rule. 'Never have sex with a married man.' George and I waited until after you two had separated, before we slept together.

LINDSAY. What do you want, the Human Rights Medal?

POPPY. I just thought if you knew that, then you mightn't feel so vengeful.

LINDSAY. Oh dear, you have got things very muddled, haven't you?

POPPY. You are so patronising to me in publications meetings.

LINDSAY. If I patronise you, which I don't, but if you feel disapproval coming from me, it's because I think many of your ideas are anti-woman.

POPPY. Anti-woman?!

LINDSAY. Unlike most of the people at the table, I still have politics.

POPPY. Feminism, you mean?

LINDSAY. I know it's a dirty word to your generation.

POPPY. You've got to be joking! You spend the entire time at
      meetings addressing your comments to the middle-aged
      men at the table. I can tell you, the younger women on
      campus find you competitive and unsupportive.

LINDSAY. The younger women on campus need to show some
      backbone. Your lot are spoilt brats as far as I'm concerned.
      I'm fed up with your incessant carping. You've been handed
      everything on a plate and you just expect the gift-giving to
      continue.

POPPY. What!?

LINDSAY. It's because your indulgent parents drove you every-
      where and gave you everything. I look at your generation of
      women and I despair. I see this obsession with glamour and
      theory. Your politics – if you have any at all – are merely an
      intellectual fashion statement.

POPPY. I thought it was just me, but it's not, is it? You're
      angry at the whole world. Angry and disappointed. And
      your precious 'politics' that you cling to, so desperately –
      it's just tired old seventies cant. I feel sorry for you.

Back on the couch, POPPY *is looking a little shell-shocked.*

LINDSAY. I had a go at writing the obituary last night. It's not
      very poetic I'm afraid. But it's a start. I just wrote down all
      the key events that I could think of. Up until the mid-nineties.

POPPY. We were married in 1998.

LINDSAY. Yes, of course you were. As I said to Bea, you are
      most welcome to have a look and add anything you think's
      important. I also thought I should go through some of his
      correspondence. It's a very important collection. I'm hoping
      we can house them in our new library. People like Susan
      Sontag and E. P. Thompson, and –

BEATRIX. He wrote to Isaac Asimov for years.

LINDSAY. Yes. And Salvador Allende.

POPPY. What new library?

LINDSAY. At the Institute of Global Studies. He had a long
      correspondence with Arthur Miller, as I recall.

BEATRIX. And there was an abusive exchange with Bob
Santamaria.

LINDSAY. Really? They were hardly soul mates, were they?
I don't think many people realised just how connected he
was with intellectuals from all over the world.

BEATRIX. Not just intellectuals.

LINDSAY. No. Writers. Artists.

BEATRIX. I had an idea. There was a poem George used to
love. It was written by an airman.

LINDSAY. A young fighter pilot.

BEATRIX. That's right. He wrote the poem on the back of a
letter to his parents, but by the time they got it, he'd been
shot down.

POPPY *looks out across the auditorium to the Island.*

LINDSAY.
Oh, I have slipped the surly bonds of earth,
And danced the skies on laughter-silvered wings . . .

BEATRIX.
And done a hundred things you have not dreamed of:
Wheeled and soared and swung –

POPPY. They don't listen to me, George. They want to write
you and me out of the picture. I won't let them archive you,
my darling. I love you. If that woman gets her way, she'll
reduce you to a man of the seventies. Yesterday's hero. And
that would be a travesty. I'll protect your work, George.
Your 'collection' of letters . . .

BEATRIX. Poppy?

POPPY. I'm sorry. I'm going home. I have some things I need
to do.

LINDSAY. Poppy.

POPPY *exits just before* DUFFY *arrives, breathlessly.*

DUFFY. I'm sorry. I've just been talking to the police. I
suppose you've heard?

LINDSAY. What about?

DUFFY. They found a body about fifty metres from the
wreckage of the plane.

BEATRIX. What?

DUFFY. There was someone else in the plane.

Silence.

LINDSAY. A woman?

DUFFY. Yes. The police don't know who it is yet, but it
appears as though she was flying the plane.

*

POPPY *is in Duffy's garage. She is tipping box after box of
papers on the floor. She is opening drawers, emptying filing
cabinets and expanding-files. She sets fire to all of George's
correspondence. Flames.*

End of Act One.

ACT TWO

Lights come up on POPPY *in George's office. The present time. The office is a mess. She is searching for something. She pulls out drawers, scans letters from his in-tray, and throws things on the floor. She is out of control. The door opens. It is* ANA.

ANA. Oh, Poppy. I'm sorry. I didn't realise –

POPPY. I was looking for some . . . papers.

ANA *takes in the devastation.*

ANA. Are you all right?

POPPY. No. Not really.

ANA. Sorry. That was a dumb question.

POPPY. I was thinking of going to Sydney for a while. I've got a friend up there. In Bondi. She's got a spare room.

ANA. That's a good idea.

POPPY. I'm certainly not hanging around for the funeral. Not now. I don't need the humiliation.

ANA. Is this about the woman – on the plane?

POPPY. Duffy's just told me. You know, I really believed that he loved me. But it was all crap, wasn't it? Everybody could see that except me. What a fool! I won't make that mistake again. No way. Because the reality is that men are cheats. They're liars and cheats. And I let my guard slip.

ANA. Don't do this to yourself.

POPPY. I've burnt all his letters.

ANA. Sorry?

POPPY. I went to Duffy's garage and I made a big bonfire.

ANA. You did what?

POPPY. You have to understand – Lindsay is doing everything she can to paint my marriage as a grotesque mistake.

ANA. You burnt my father's letters?

POPPY. Listen, Lindsay is evil.

ANA. Like the ones from Susan Sontag? Marshall McLuhan? All those letters?

POPPY. I had to protect his reputation.

ANA. Oh, you can't have.

POPPY. It's okay, Ana.

ANA. No! No, it isn't. This is unbelievable! Does Lindsay know?

POPPY. What's it matter?

ANA. Tell me!

POPPY. You don't understand.

ANA. Tell me!

POPPY. I don't know.

> ANA *exits.* POPPY *escapes to her memory. The kitchen of the Carlton house, 1999.*

> What is it? Tell me.

GEORGE. Lindsay has just offered me a promotion.

POPPY. A promotion? Yeah, sure.

GEORGE. She did! She called me into her office this afternoon and she says sweetly –

> LINDSAY *enters George's office.*

> 'I've heard that you have some misgivings about the Institute of Global Studies?'

POPPY. That was an understatement. Have you seen their web site? (*To the audience.*) 'The Institute of Global Studies is the realisation of a dynamic partnership between the University and Brasch Industries. It's the vision of Dwight

Brasch, President of Brasch Industries. A privately-funded
institute which targets students at the top-end of the market –
clients prepared to make a financial commitment to excellence.' Which means students pay full fees.

GEORGE. My primary misgiving is that it's fundamentally
undemocratic. You're reviving private privilege at the very
moment we were poised to make it a thing of the past.
You're building an institute for the sons and daughters of
the rich – right here in the heart of a public university.
By all means – go and build your corporate college in the
hills or on the bloody Gold Coast. But to build it here –
Lindsay – you know it will suck this public institution dry.

POPPY (*to the audience*). 'The Institute of Global Studies is
like a huge aeroplane. In this plane we are doing away with
economy class. We are doing away with business class.
In this aeroplane, which is about to roar down the runway
and take off into the future, we have only one class, ladies
and gentlemen – first class. From one end of the plane to
the other. This is a first-class institution. That is the Dwight
Brasch vision.'

LINDSAY. I'm surprised that your unreconstructed Marxism is
still popular with the students.

GEORGE. This is not Marxism. This is about core values.

LINDSAY. The fact is, we'll be offering a lot of scholarships.

GEORGE. Scholarships! Come off it. Don't tell me you're
peddling that crap.

LINDSAY. George, none of the really clever kids will miss out.
You have to see that.

GEORGE. You'll let a handful of poor kids over the drawbridge?
Is that it? And when those kids make it, the conservative
elite say, 'See?! Regardless of class, anyone in this country
is able to achieve success if they sweat at it.' And if some
kid from the western suburbs can do well, why can't all of
them? And there follows the great conservative lie: 'It must
be because all the others are lazy and unmotivated. They
don't know the meaning of hard work.'

LINDSAY. George, this is not denying an opportunity to a single person, you realise. This is an addition to the University, which will go on playing its public role as it's always done. It's not like the money's being siphoned off from some other activity. This is money we would not have otherwise, if it wasn't for –

GEORGE. This is money for which we pay a crippling price.

LINDSAY. George. There are principles at stake – I understand that. That's why the Institute needs leadership – a quality of direction which only you could bring to it. I want to offer you the inaugural Chair of Global Studies. It'll be a whole new beginning for you.

LINDSAY *holds up a set of keys.*

GEORGE. They bought you a sportscar?

LINDSAY. No. They bought you a plane.

GEORGE. You're joking.

LINDSAY. It's waiting for you on the runway at Moorabbin.

GEORGE. Yeah?

LINDSAY *tosses the keys to* GEORGE. GEORGE *catches them deftly. He smiles.*

Whose idea is this?

LINDSAY. Dwight Brasch.

GEORGE. The great man himself?

LINDSAY. Yes.

GEORGE. Can I speak to him?

LINDSAY. Why not? He's waiting on your call. (*She punches Brasch's number into a phone.*) Dwight Brasch please. Lindsay Graham. I've got Professor George with me. He'd like a word. Thanks.

GEORGE. Mr Brasch. How are you? . . . Very well, thank you . . . Yes. She's put me in the picture . . . Yes. It's come as a bolt from the blue . . . No. Complete surprise . . . Mmm hmm . . . Comrade Brasch, what ruthless bastards like you don't understand, is that people like me can't be silenced. We're not for sale. We're not tempted. Not for an instant.

He hangs up and throws the keys back. LINDSAY *catches them.*

Keep your eye on the altimeter, Lin. If you fly too low, you're dead.

He returns to his conversation with POPPY.

POPPY. What kind of an aeroplane?

GEORGE. A Cessna 172. Brand new. Better than Duffy's. Bastards.

POPPY. Shit.

GEORGE. Two hundred and fifty thousand dollars worth. (*Beat.*) There was a time when Lindsay was really out there – making a difference. She had the heart of a reformer, you know. She wrote that beautiful radical thesis. She was President of the SRC, heavily involved in Vietnam demos, the Springbok protests. She organised the sit-ins outside the South African Embassy in the mid-seventies.

POPPY. This is why baby boomers suck. For all the misty-eyed reminiscence about demos and crusades and sit-ins – they were just dance parties without the dancing. I mean, let's face it. You could believe it meant something, if that generation were setting a different political agenda now. But they're not.

GEORGE. Well, that's true.

POPPY. I bet that Lindsay thinks her rise up the career ladder is a blow for feminism. Every time she gets a salary hike she accepts it on behalf of all women. As a political act. Professor Lindsay Graham. Role model.

GEORGE *puts his arms around her.*

GEORGE. I think you should keep that very quiet.

They kiss.

POPPY. You're the exception, George. Most people would take the plane. In fact most people would think you're a fool.

GEORGE. What about you?

POPPY. Before I met you, I would have taken the plane.

GEORGE disappears. POPPY re-enters the present. She surveys the devastation and begins to pack it up. LINDSAY bursts in.

LINDSAY. What have you done? I've been looking everywhere for you.

POPPY continues sorting through his papers.

POPPY. What's it to you?

LINDSAY. For Chris'sake, girl. Stop it! Stop it immediately!

POPPY. How dare you lord it over me like this!

LINDSAY. You haven't seen anything yet. You're lucky I didn't call the police.

POPPY. Yeah. Right. The hero of the Springbok demos calls in the pigs!

LINDSAY. You're trespassing. This is not your property. These are not your things.

POPPY. They belong to my husband.

LINDSAY. I hope you've got a good lawyer. That's all I can say. Because you're in deep shit. Do you understand that? What you have done is not just arson. Oh, no! You didn't just burn down any old garage.

POPPY. I don't know what you're talking about.

LINDSAY. I have nightmares about people like you. People who are so ignorant and narcissistic. Who have so little grasp of the value of anything, that they could destroy documents of such profound value. I know you have no respect for history, but George was an historian. Marrying you was the greatest mistake of his life. And I know he regretted it. Bitterly.

POPPY. You know nothing, Lindsay.

LINDSAY. Why do you think he was flirting with every woman on campus? Why do you think he was sneaking off for secret weekends on the Island? Is that the act of a man who's happily married? I don't think so. You were just a pretty little toy, that he badly wished he'd never picked up.

POPPY. The man is dead. Can't you leave it?

LINDSAY. I suppose you imagine that your own thoughts on the state of the nation are as interesting and valuable as those of Robert Lucas, for example. He won a Nobel Prize for Economics. His correspondence was in the collection. As I recall. But what does that matter? When the world has your diaries. I'm hoping you've saved them. You didn't burn them, did you? Because that would be a real travesty.

POPPY. No wonder the staff and students hate you so much.

LINDSAY. Don't you get it? George was a hero, around here. And you've just destroyed his legacy.

POPPY *exits.* LINDSAY *calls after her.*

You'll go to jail for this.

*

ANA *cuts across the space in the present. She is carrying a plastic garbage bag. She picks up a small amount of dust and lets it slip through her fingers.* BEATRIX *observes.*

BEATRIX. Ana. What are you doing?

ANA. Your husband's ashes.

BEATRIX. Ana.

ANA. This is every letter my father wrote. And all the correspondence he received in the course of his life.

BEATRIX. Oh, my God. Did you do this?

ANA. Me? Do you think I am that morally bankrupt?

ANA *enters her memory space. It is 1997. George's office.*

GEORGE. So you want to go Switzerland – to meditate.

ANA. Yes.

GEORGE. Why can't you meditate here?

ANA. Because people from all over the world are gathering in Lugano to meditate for world peace.

GEORGE. And how does that work? Do you think? I give you two thousand dollars. You sit on a mountain in Switzerland, with your eyes closed, and suddenly Saddam Hussein decides to invite members of the UN on a personal tour of his weapon storage sites?

ANA. People have to transform from within before any kind of social change is possible.

GEORGE. And that's what you believe? Is it?

ANA. I don't think world peace can be achieved without individuals being at peace with themselves.

GEORGE. Right. So you want a cheque for two thousand dollars.

ANA. Yes.

GEORGE. As a gesture towards world peace?

Pause.

ANA. Yes.

GEORGE. Okay.

He gets out his cheque book.

ANA. Some people say that meditation is the only true revolutionary act.

GEORGE *writes the cheque. He looks up.*

GEORGE. Personally, I think meditation is a clear example of political impotence. Just as the band played while the *Titanic* went down. For people to survive they have to take action. They have to organise. (*Offering her the cheque.*) There you are. Two thousand dollars.

ANA (*taking the cheque*). Thank you. (*Reading it.*) Amnesty
International.

She puts the cheque back on his desk.

(*Turning to leave.*) Thanks for helping me, Dad.

GEORGE. Ana. I don't understand what it is that you believe in.
What matters to you?

ANA. I've just told you.

GEORGE. Meditation, you mean.

ANA. Yes.

GEORGE. Chanting?

ANA. Yes.

GEORGE. But to what end?

ANA. Look. I'm not interested in articulating a belief
structure.

GEORGE. Why not? What does interest you? Apart from
chanting and omming?

ANA. I don't want to talk about this with you.

GEORGE. You read voraciously, but you refuse to go to
university. You play the piano, but you don't want to be a
musician. Your mother tells me you compose music. But,
of course, you would never consider playing publicly.

ANA. I'm sorry I'm so disappointing.

GEORGE. Look, I know that the fashion is a kind of ironic
detachment, which both you children seem to have in
spades. But I really don't know where that takes you, Ana,
except despair.

ANA. Yes. You're quite right. Despair is a good word for it.

She exits.

*

BEATRIX (*addressing the audience*). I finally got through to Rajasthan – to Jaipur, where my son lives. They're expecting him back tomorrow apparently. He's been away. David's a photographer. He's doing this series on washing – all over Asia; photographing clothes lines. He and George have always had such a turbulent time. I remember when we first came to Australia, we were living in Box Hill. David was about five. There was this giant cottonwood tree in the front garden. It must have been about twenty metres high. Huge thing. Anyway, one day I couldn't find him and there he was, right up the top of the tree. Terrified. He couldn't get down. So I called George at the Uni and he came rushing home and we ended up having to get the fire brigade. It was a big drama. And we were all quite shaken up by it. But the very next day David climbed the tree again. I couldn't believe it. He was waiting up there when George got home. George was livid. He was shouting with rage and frustration and we were on the verge of ringing the fire brigade again. Then David just climbed down. Methodically. Branch by branch. George was always so hard on him. For all his democratic ideals, when it came to his own boy, he was a Stalinist. He was. And David, unfortunately, was an anarchist. From the moment he was born. He was just defiant. And he's been like that all his life. Not aggressive. Just quietly resistant to authority. George said it was my fault. That I had no understanding of the importance of discipline. George never found a way of getting close to him.

*

BEATRIX *enters her memory. We revisit the scene from Act One, where* BEATRIX *goes to see* GEORGE *in 1998, before she leaves for San Gimignano. George's study.*

GEORGE. I've got something for you.

He indicates a painting resting against a filing cabinet. It is facing away from view. It is the nude of BEATRIX, *painted by Arthur Boyd.*

BEATRIX. Don't you want it anymore?

GEORGE. I love that painting, Bea. I've always loved it. I just thought you might like to take it with you. To San Gimignano.

BEATRIX *scrutinises him for a moment.*

I was thinking of hanging it here, but after all the fuss about sexual harassment in universities, perhaps it's not appropriate to have a nude in your office. Even if it is of your first wife.

BEATRIX. It's not appropriate to keep it at your house, I take it?

GEORGE. No.

BEATRIX. Your little friend is moving in, is she?

GEORGE. Her name is Poppy.

BEATRIX. Hmm. I've always thought it rather odd that Lindsay was happy to live in that house with this (*the painting*) in the living room.

GEORGE. Lindsay is very clinical in the way she allocates her emotions. This is art. Very valuable art.

BEATRIX. What about Poppy?

GEORGE. No comparison. Poppy looked at the painting and she said, 'If I had tits as beautiful as those, you could keep the painting.' She's incredible, Bea. Truly. You know she edits a magazine on the web? She has just persuaded Umberto Eco to write for her, next month.

BEATRIX. Umberto Eco?

GEORGE. Impressive, eh? (*Beat.*) She put out her first edition, last year. It's called *DIRT*. Her editorial was brilliant – a really original take on postmodernism. She called it 'Buddy, Can You Spare a Paradigm?'.

BEATRIX. *DIRT?* Very . . . witty.

GEORGE. Oh, come on, Bea.

BEATRIX. She's a child.

GEORGE. She's like a beacon of positive energy. She's bright and sassy. I feel transformed when I'm with her. She's ambitious, but she's not driven and dried up by it all.

BEATRIX. She's twenty-nine.

GEORGE. You're hung-up on this age thing.

BEATRIX. Ana says Poppy is a 'geek girl with attitude'. Is that praise?

GEORGE. From Ana? Sure.

BEATRIX. So she's a new kind of girl. Every generation produces them, you know – the girl who somehow embodies the spirit of the times. I don't have a clue what it means, 'geek girl' for God sake. But it is curious. What you're doing with this girl doesn't make me feel old or jealous or cheated. It just makes me want to be with people who know the words to Joni Mitchell songs.

GEORGE. Oh, Bea. Still the same.

BEATRIX. You realise you're risking a lot. Don't you? People our age don't really approve of their peers going off and having affairs with young girls.

GEORGE. I'm not very interested in what people 'our age' think.

BEATRIX. From the outside it looks so foolish. So clichéd. For one thing, you're leaving Lindsay out in the cold to face a very lonely old age. I just can't believe that you would be so callous. I suppose it's none of my business.

GEORGE. Why are you siding with Lindsay all of a sudden?

BEATRIX. I don't think you understand. Something happens to older women. After fifty we become invisible. Men just look straight through us. So the idea that, when you're feeling most vulnerable, you might be rejected by your husband, passed over for a younger, newer, shinier model, is just too painful.

GEORGE. I'm really quite sure, Bea, that Lindsay doesn't feel invisible.

BEATRIX. Well, that's very convenient then.

GEORGE. She's at the height of her powers. (*Pause.*) I don't believe it, Bea. I don't believe that you feel invisible.

BEATRIX. It's one of the reasons I'm moving to Italy. They love and respect their women over there.

Silence.

It's just that I'm going away. I might not see you for a few years. I don't want to leave thinking that you're –

GEORGE. What?

Pause.

BEATRIX. – creating this mess. I can't give you my blessing. And I would really like to be able to do that, George. To wish you well. Before I go.

*

BEATRIX *returns to the present. She stops at the mirror and regards herself.* ANA *watches her mother.*

ANA (*to the audience*). I remember when Dad and Poppy got married. Two years ago. I was in Barcelona – thank Christ. Dad rang me one night, about 3 a.m. and he said –

A spotlight snaps onto GEORGE *on the phone.*

GEORGE. Do you think Lindsay feels invisible?

ANA (*on the phone*). Lindsay? Excuse me?

GEORGE. Your mother says that middle-aged women become invisible.

ANA. That sounds like Mum. She's always liked being looked at. When all the feminists were carrying on about men on building sites wolf-whistling, Mum was worried about how she'd cope when they stopped. She's really quite vain, you know.

They laugh.

And, what's more, she's got no politics. We went to see *My Brilliant Career* and she was really disappointed. She wanted Judy Davis to go off with Sam Neill at the end.

GEORGE'*s spotlight snaps off.* ANA *puts down the phone.*

(*To the audience.*) We both laughed and I felt disgusted with myself. He'd tricked me into being disloyal.

*

BEATRIX. I need to get my hair cut. We should both go. Just for a treat. You know, I was thinking, Ana, you should try a little bob. Just for fun. It'd look gorgeous. Very gamin. I think that's the look you should go for.

ANA. I am really happy with my hair. Just as it is. Thanks.

BEATRIX. Okay. I just thought it would be fun.

ANA. You're like one of those salesgirls. They hold up a dress and say, 'What about this? This is fun.' And you want to say, 'It's a piece of clothing, you moron. An inanimate object. It is not, of its own accord, fun.'

Pause.

BEATRIX. You don't seem to me to know what fun is.

ANA. Well, it's not playing dress-ups and going to the hair-dresser with your mother. That's for sure. (*Beat.*) I'm going out for a while.

*

DUFFY *enters. He is at home.*

DUFFY (*to the audience*). George never recovered from losing his kids. Bea took them to England. She sent David off to Rugby. You know Rugby School? Where *Tom Brown's Schooldays* was set. I think it was her old man's idea. Anyway, he forked out for it. George was furious. As far as he was concerned –

In DUFFY*'s memory:*

GEORGE. She's turning my son into Lord Foppington. Poncing about with all those ruling-class snots. Don't I have any rights at all, Duff? I'm the boy's father, for Chris'sake.

DUFFY. What did Bea say?

GEORGE. She said that I'd forfeited my rights, by leaving her.

DUFFY. She left you.

GEORGE. Yeah. Well. I'm the one having the affair.

DUFFY. Yes. There is that.

GEORGE. They're breeding grounds of cruelty, you know –
English public schools. If the ruling class know anything,
they know how to be exquisite bullies. The only way to
survive is to develop a contempt for weakness. Even the
weak themselves develop it. They end up fuelled by their
own self-loathing.

DUFFY. David's not weak.

GEORGE. Yes, he is. He doesn't believe in himself. He doesn't
believe in anything. (*Beat.*) Neither of them do.

DUFFY (*to the audience*). I often thought Rugby was the
making of David. I'd never say this to George, but I actually
thought he blossomed. He became a sort of gentle eccentric,
in a way that would have been impossible for him here in
Australia. At that time anyway.

*

POPPY *enters.*

DUFFY. I'm assuming you don't want to speak at the funeral?

POPPY. No.

Pause.

DUFFY. Lindsay rang me this morning. She said she'd like
someone from the University to say a few words.

POPPY. Someone like Lindsay herself?

DUFFY. How would you feel if Lindsay were to say a few
words? Not as his ex-wife. Of course. But in her capacity
as the Dean of the Faculty.

POPPY. I'd feel sick.

DUFFY. I thought you might.

POPPY *enters her memory. It is 1998.* GEORGE *bursts into
the kitchen and heads for the phone.*

GEORGE. This is unbelievable! Where did you hear this?

POPPY. Professor Dubois.

GEORGE. Dear God. (*Into the phone.*) Lindsay? . . . George. You're closing down the French Department now? What's going on? (*Beat.*) Of course it's my business, what are you talking about? You want me to look the other way while you vandalise the Arts Faculty . . . I'm coming over. I'll be there in ten minutes. (*He hangs up.*) French, for Chris'sake.

POPPY. George!

GEORGE. What?

POPPY. I made this. For our dinner.

She shows him a pot. He looks in.

GEORGE. Is it liver cleansing?

POPPY. Kidney bean casserole.

They look at each other with mutual lack of enthusiasm.

GEORGE. How about I meet you at Poppolino's? Say eight-thirty?

POPPY. You are incorrigible!

GEORGE. And you are gorgeous.

GEORGE *embraces her and then exits.* LINDSAY *enters her office. She addresses the audience.*

LINDSAY. He was incorrigible. Infuriating. The situation, as I'm sure you're well aware –

GEORGE *enters.* LINDSAY *enters her memory. 1999.*

What?

GEORGE. You talk about this as though it were a *fait accompli.*

LINDSAY. It is a *fait accompli.* The Faculty has a two-million-dollar operating deficit. By the year 2005 your Department will be half a million dollars in debt. The time has come to think carefully about income-generating activities.

GEORGE. Perhaps we could have an interdepartmental sausage sizzle?

LINDSAY. This is serious, George. I'm talking about consulting work or partnerships with private enterprise. I'm afraid you're going to have to renounce your tribal hostility to the corporate sector.

GEORGE. That, I'm afraid, is impossible. You may well do their bidding. I will not.

LINDSAY. You don't have a lot of choice, George. The consultant's report has identified the History Department as one of the 'non-performing' sectors. Within twelve months you're looking at slashing a quarter of your subjects and sacking five or six Senior Lecturers. And that's optimistic. You're not getting the clients.

GEORGE. My enrolments are up.

LINDSAY. But most of your students don't pay fees.

GEORGE. Oh, so we should be teaching tourism, marketing and hospitality management?

LINDSAY. Your elitism doesn't wash anymore, George.

GEORGE. Elitism, is it? You used to call it academic excellence.

LINDSAY. Look. Students want practical and applied knowledge. They want vocational training. The days of ancient Greek and Latin are over. It's just nostalgia.

GEORGE. That's your trump card. Nostalgia? That's your way of deflecting any criticism. 'It's just nostalgia. Fear of change. On the part of old-style academics.' While you go about blithely dismantling everything the University stands for –

LINDSAY. You and I both know that, taught well, the vocational subject can have the same transformational power as the traditional discipline.

GEORGE. You and I both know that that is complete hogwash. You seriously want me to believe that the natural place to seek answers to the riddles of human existence is to be found in tourism policy? I don't think so. You've stopped thinking about them as students. This is the issue here. They're all customers to you. You're a middle manager with a marketing brief: How can I make this university more like a shopping mall?

LINDSAY. My brief is about survival.

GEORGE. Oh, you'll survive all right. Managers and cockroaches –

LINDSAY. I'm talking about the survival of the University! The trouble with you, George, is that you refuse to take responsibility for the future.

GEORGE. There are many possible futures, Lindsay. You don't have a monopoly on that. But let's get real here – you're the one jeopardising the survival of the institution.

LINDSAY. No, you get real. In the first place, you can't just turn your back on what students want to learn, because they'll just go elsewhere.

GEORGE. Good. Because your customer-oriented marketing posture means that the least intellectually challenging course is privileged every time. It doesn't make sense to ask a first-year if we should be teaching postcolonial history because she doesn't know what it is yet. She's not yet in possession of the knowledge to make that decision. But you're obsessed with pandering to her demands.

LINDSAY. Her demands are fairly straightforward, George. She wants a job at the end of it.

GEORGE. You want to turn our students into corporate fodder. You've lost sight of the function of a university to produce educated citizens. Not just compliant employees.

LINDSAY. Oh, for Chris'sake, George. How can you be so simplistic?

GEORGE. Can't you see? Your agenda is being driven by management clones. I've seen them on planes. Up there in business class. They're all reading Wilbur Smith.

LINDSAY. Exactly. And they won't fund courses about Molière or Plato or the history of medieval Spain.

GEORGE. They don't believe in anything outside the business paradigm.

LINDSAY. Tell me about it.

GEORGE. Lindsay, you're ushering in the Dark Ages. No, worse. At least in the Dark Ages, there were monasteries where scholarship and learning were carried on.

LINDSAY. Within twelve months, I would say, it is highly likely that your Department will close. What are your strategies, George?

GEORGE. That's the wrong question, Professor. You ask, 'How do we implement the corporate agenda?' The real question is: 'How do we fight it?'

GEORGE exits.

*

The corridor outside the Arts Faculty office. LINDSAY is surveying some damage to the building and the assembly of students outside. ANA and BEATRIX approach.

BEATRIX. What's happening?

LINDSAY. We've had to cut down some elm trees to make way for the Institute of Global Studies.

ANA. I saw the graffiti: 'Think global, fuck local'.

LINDSAY. It's usually more personalised. 'Professor Graham is a philistine'. 'Graham is a fascist'. That sort of thing.

ANA (*to the audience*). This is the woman whose Ph.D. thesis was called 'Manning the Barricades'. Mind you, when she got heavily into feminism she snuck into the library and changed the name to 'Our Day at the Barricades'.

LINDSAY. Let's get this funeral organised, shall we?

She gets out a file and puts it on her desk. ANA takes a deep breath.

ANA. Lindsay, I'm sorry to have to tell you this, but Poppy has destroyed all of Dad's correspondence.

LINDSAY. Yes.

ANA. You know?

LINDSAY. Oh, yes. It's with the lawyers at the moment. I'm going to press charges.

ANA. Oh. Good.

Pause.

BEATRIX. What's the legal situation? I was thinking that perhaps they were hers to burn?

ANA. They were not hers.

LINDSAY. I'm afraid, true to form, George didn't bother about a will.

BEATRIX. Oh, God.

ANA. He didn't leave a will?

LINDSAY. People who believe they're immortal, always die intestate.

BEATRIX. Well, the letters are probably Poppy's then. Aren't they? She's his wife.

LINDSAY. It's more complex than that. We'll be arguing that they're the intellectual property of the University. (*To* ANA) Are you okay?

ANA. Yep.

BEATRIX. What's up, darling?

ANA. Nothing.

Long pause.

BEATRIX. Is it the letters?

ANA *is unable to speak.*

LINDSAY. I think the most important thing is to make Poppy understand that it'd be best for everyone if she didn't attend the funeral.

BEATRIX. Lindsay. She is George's wife. You must stop treating her as an interloper.

LINDSAY. I'm treating her as a criminal, actually. But what I'm saying is that people at the funeral will feel nothing for that girl, except contempt.

BEATRIX. I think you're underestimating people.

ANA. She doesn't want to come. She told me. She feels humiliated about him having an affair.

BEATRIX. If it's true.

ANA. Of course it's true. He really didn't care about any of us. Not me. Not you. Not Poppy. None of us. Face it. The man did not care. As for the funeral. I don't know why you're bothering. Because I'm not. I'm not even going to be there.

ANA *exits.*

*

POPPY *is on the St Kilda pier with* DUFFY.

POPPY. I've gone over it again and again, trying to remember the intensity of the feeling, because I didn't doubt for a moment. I went straight to your garage and I did it. But now I just feel numb.

DUFFY. Mmm.

POPPY. George believed so deeply that Lindsay was wrong.

DUFFY. I know.

POPPY. Brasch Industries. The Institute of Global Studies. It was all immoral.

DUFFY. Yes.

POPPY. And to think that she would have the audacity and lack of ethics to use his reputation . . . when he was dead, when he couldn't fight back. So I fought it for him. That was the idea. I really wanted to do the right thing, Duff. But now, it just looks like a shabby little act of revenge, on the part of a jealous wife.

*

The present. ANA *and* LINDSAY *are having a coffee together.*

ANA. I had this dream the other night that Dad was being knighted by the Queen. For his services to History. Or something.

LINDSAY. That'd be the day.

ANA. And Poppy was there wearing a black pill-box hat and a white suit and she had four little boys with her. They all looked the same. Like quadruplets. And she had them on this retractable lead. Four little boys in matching sailor suits. Anyway, Dad made this speech and he said, 'I want to thank my family. My wife Poppy. And my sons Billy, Tommy, Hughey and Jerry.' Whatever their names were. And Mum and I and David were standing at the back of the hall. But he didn't mention us. We didn't exist.

LINDSAY. Ana. He loved you. With all his heart. You must believe me. He really cared about you.

ANA. But not enough to make provision for us in a will.

LINDSAY. I honestly don't think it occurred to him that he might die.

ANA. He was fifty-eight.

LINDSAY. That's not so old.

*

DUFFY *is sitting at his kitchen table, reading the paper, when* BEATRIX *arrives.*

DUFFY. Thanks for coming, Bea.

BEATRIX. You got your instructions all right? The running order and everything?

DUFFY. Yes. Got everything. She runs a tight ship, our Lindsay. (*Pause.*) Did you see her obituary today in the paper?

BEATRIX. Yes.

DUFFY. She omitted any mention of Poppy. This is a vendetta, Bea. It's got to stop. The girl is delirious with grief. Her husband's dead. She's being vilified by everybody and now she's tormented by the fact that George died in the company of some woman she doesn't know.

BEATRIX. What do you think, Duff? Do you think he was cheating on her too?

Pause.

DUFFY. It doesn't look good.

Pause.

BEATRIX. Look after yourself.

BEATRIX *kisses him gently on the forehead.*

DUFFY. You too.

BEATRIX *exits.*

(*To the audience.*) One time, I remember, we drove down to North Point, on the Island, because someone told us they'd seen some whales. There must have been about thirty. Diving and spurting and mucking around out there in the Strait. And we got talking to this timber worker who'd brought his son to look. Trev, his name was. A real redneck – mouthing off about unions and blacks and tree-hugging greenies. And I'm thinking, how are we going to give this bloke the flick? But not George. He wanted some fishing tips. So that night, the four of us stood on the edge of a beach at the bottom of the world and we fished . . . with these great rods in the air. And at midnight . . . we built a fire on the beach . . . and fried up the fish . . . and knocked back a few beers. And this man Trev, and his boy . . . they talked. To George really. Cutting timber was all that bloke knew, but he'd been out of work for almost a year. And he was only just hanging on. But as the sun rose, and we packed up our things, I could see that this bloke was feeling stronger. He felt he'd been heard. He felt closer to his boy. That night's like a light in the darkness for me. George did that for people. I taught him to fly. Did you know? I taught him. But George, mate, George. You taught me to live.

*

POPPY *is on the St Kilda Pier. A fisherman,* GEORGE, *is fishing nearby.* BEATRIX *approaches.*

BEATRIX. Poppy. (*Pause.*) I have something to show you. This is a letter which didn't get burnt because it's been in my handbag. George sent this to me in San Gimignano, the day before your wedding.

GEORGE *turns.*

'I think you'd like her, Bea.'

GEORGE. 'I want you – of all the people in this world – to know that this is not the folly of a middle-aged man. She is everything I thought I would mistrust: an individualist, a postmodern cyber-chick. But she's everything I know I want. Headstrong, brave, beautiful of course, and as open-minded as the sunrise. She thinks in different ways. What I mistrusted as her lack of politics is actually a truly radical sensibility. At the core of her being she is genuinely open to the possibilities for change. And yes – she was my post-graduate student. But I didn't fall in love with her over her thesis. I bumped into her one night on St Kilda pier. Fishing. The postmodern girl – sitting there on a summer's night in shorts and a grotty T-shirt, with a plastic bucket and three dead fish. You can see why I was smitten. So be happy for me, Bea. Say a prayer to your Tuscan god for both of us. I never dared to hope that I should pass this way again. Your loving ex – '

BEATRIX. ' – George.' (*She folds the letter, and removes her glasses.*) I just wanted to remind you of how much he loved you.

*

Later, in Ana's flat.

ANA. I don't understand you sometimes, Mum. I know you've made another life. You've got Raffy and you have a lovely time together in San Gim. But doesn't it hurt just a little bit? I mean, why would Dad write to you about how much he loved another woman? I don't get it. (*Pause.*) Don't you

want him to say that the day he left was the most stupid
thing he's ever done and he's regretted it for the rest of his
life?

BEATRIX. Why do you want him to say that?

ANA (*through tears*). Because you're my mother. Isn't that
what every kid wants – whose parents are divorced?

BEATRIX. Ana –

ANA. Don't. I know what you're going to say. Most people get
over it by the time they're twenty-eight, right? (*Pause.*) I
don't know why I can't get over it.

BEATRIX. Ana, I didn't read her the whole letter.

She hands the letter to ANA.

*

Lindsay's office. LINDSAY *is daydreaming.* GEORGE *appears
at the window. It is 1979.*

LINDSAY. What are you doing here?

GEORGE. I'm bored.

LINDSAY. Really, for an academic you have the concentration
span of a gnat.

GEORGE. That's because I know you're just down the
corridor. You're going to have to change universities. It's
impossible. I can't work.

LINDSAY. Maybe we could go home for lunch.

GEORGE. I thought we could go to Port Fairy, actually.

LINDSAY. Now?

GEORGE. Tomorrow. But we'll have to get someone to feed
Beatrix's dog.

There is a knock at the door. GEORGE *vanishes.* LINDSAY
returns reluctantly to the present.

LINDSAY. Yes? (*Pause.*) Duffy. Come in.

DUFFY. I'm sorry to disturb. I know you're busy.

LINDSAY. I was daydreaming actually. Do you remember that fishing holiday the four of us took in Port Fairy? You and Nell? George and I? When was that?

DUFFY. I don't know. 1979, maybe.

LINDSAY. Are you okay?

DUFFY. They've identified the woman in the plane. (*Pause.*) It was Rachel.

Pause.

LINDSAY. Rachel.

DUFFY. I'm so sorry.

The door opens and a furious GEORGE *bursts on the scene.* LINDSAY *is engulfed by her memory. It is 1999.*

GEORGE. I need to talk to you.

LINDSAY. What about?

GEORGE *is waving a letter.*

GEORGE. This young woman – Rachel – has written me a letter. To tell me that I am her father. And you are her mother. And that she has made contact with you, but you are not ready to see her yet. Is this true? Lindsay? Lindsay?

LINDSAY *nods.*

Answer me.

LINDSAY. How dare they do this! You enter into it on the understanding that the confidentiality will never be broken.

GEORGE. You had a baby. My baby.

LINDSAY. This is the most profound betrayal of trust.

GEORGE. Oh, you're telling me. (*Pause.*) I am assuming that this is why you went to Sydney to finish your Ph.D. Hmm? I am assuming that this happened as a result of that one night. Yes?

LINDSAY. Mmm.

GEORGE. After we went to see Gough at the Town Hall. And then we went to the front bar at Stewart's?

LINDSAY. Mmm.

GEORGE. And after that, we went back to your house in Parkville?

LINDSAY *nods.*

Once.

Long pause.

And then, you and I were married for ten years and never once did you feel able to tell me that you and I had a daughter.

LINDSAY. I got pregnant two months before Ana was born.

GEORGE. Don't tell me that. Don't you think I can do the maths? Jesus Christ.

LINDSAY. What choice did I have?

GEORGE. You had the obvious one. The screaming, fucking, obvious one.

LINDSAY. That's not true. You've forgotten. Abortion wasn't even legal. And I couldn't –

GEORGE. Not that. I'm not talking about abortion, for Chris'sake. I'm talking about the choice you made, not to tell me.

Pause.

LINDSAY. You were so ashamed of what we did, that if I told you that we'd also made a baby –

GEORGE. What?

LINDSAY. I don't know what. But it would have been the end of us.

GEORGE. You've kept this secret for twenty-seven years, Lindsay.

Silence.

Wasn't there any occasion, any moment of intimacy or tenderness or trust, when you felt you could tell me this?

Silence.

Does it occur to you that our entire marriage was based on fraudulence?

*

ANA (*reading*).
   'Dearest Bea,
   My first and loveliest wife. I am filled today with a sense of how blessed I have been. To have been known and held and loved by so astonishing a woman.'

GEORGE *takes over.*

GEORGE. 'We grew up together, you and I. I look back now and see the girl and boy we were in Paris – filled with the magic of that city and the exhilaration of the times. The academic, the painter, the mother, the father. The travellers, the immigrants. The outsiders. And eventually, the Australians. I loved you as much as any man could love a woman. But it came to an end – and the fault was mine or yours – however you want to tell it.

Our girl is sad, and perhaps we made her so. Our boy is a rover, and we never really know whether we gave birth to a traveller or a drifter.

This is the universe in which I have lived. Making do. Married for a second time to a steel-bright woman who never quite has time. And every evening – have I ever told you this – I have walked your dog Constable. (Whatever possessed you to call it that?!) Yes, walked your old, slow, brown-eyed dog through the pathways of Royal Park and round beyond the zoo. I see myself at a distance. Professor George and his first wife's yellow dog – walking lonely in the park.

Well, my love, mother of my children, deserter of Constable . . . I am to be married. I am to wait at the altar, a third and final time. And I know that in the eyes of some – ladies who lunch, disappointed divorcees and fornicating pharmacists

who gaze in judgement on the street – in the eyes of these –
I shall seem a fool. But hell is other people. And I am me.
And she is she. So be happy for me, Bea. Say a prayer to
your Tuscan god for both of us. Because, my love, I never
dared to hope that I should pass this way again.'

Silence.

ANA. 'Our girl is sad.' At the end of the story, in all the hundreds
of thousands of words my father wrote, that's it. 'Our girl is
sad. And perhaps we made her so.' I didn't expect to be a
topic of conversation in his letters to Milton Friedman or
Manning Clark, but in a letter to my mother – That's it, then.

*

DUFFY *and* LINDSAY *are sitting in a bar. It is late at night.*

LINDSAY. How many times did George see her? Rachel.

DUFFY. I'm not sure. (*Pause.*) Two or three.

LINDSAY. He didn't tell me.

DUFFY. You didn't want to know.

LINDSAY. Of course I did. Her first letter arrived on the day
I was inaugurated as Dean. I couldn't deal with it, Duff.
I put the letter in the back of my cupboard and I thought –
I just have to wait for the right time. And then, the following
September, I took a week off and I tried to write to her. That
was a black week, I tell you. And when I got back to work,
I had these crippling panic attacks. So I knew I had to make
a choice. I'd have to resign and deal with my demons or
commit myself to being the Dean of the Arts Faculty. So
I cut her out of my life. Again. All the time I'm asking
myself – what is the appropriate course of action for
someone in my position, and I end up comparing myself
to some fictitious man, doing my job. How would he cope,
if this had happened to him? And I know that he would bury
his pain and get on with it. That's why you get paid good
money, because people trust that you'll put the job first.

DUFFY *nods. He enters his memory. He and* GEORGE *are
together at the Island, six months ago.*

GEORGE. I just don't understand, Duff, how she could be so callous? It's not normal.

DUFFY. Some women just don't have maternal feelings.

GEORGE. This is more than maternal feelings. This is about an essential morality, isn't it? There's a kid out there who's in real pain and Lindsay and I are largely responsible. There's no getting around that. And she, more than me, fuck it! I didn't even know. But she has just turned her back. What kind of a woman is that?

DUFFY. What would you have done if you'd known? Hmm? All those years ago? Would you have said to Bea, 'You know, while you were seven months pregnant, I was having sex with an extremely beautiful woman and she got pregnant. So, unfortunately, I have to do the right thing and marry her? Sorry.' Or would you have said to Lindsay, 'Go away and do whatever you have to do. If you need money – I'll help you, but I never want to see you again.' Because that's what she feared. Don't you see? She was so in love with you.

DUFFY *returns to the present.*

LINDSAY. Why do you think she wanted to see me? Rachel?

DUFFY. She was getting married.

LINDSAY. Oh, God.

DUFFY. To a farmer from Wangaratta.

LINDSAY. Poor man.

Pause.

DUFFY. Yes.

LINDSAY. That's it then. My husband and my daughter. Both dead. So that's all there is now. More of the same. More work. That's all there is. (*Beat.*) They've offered me the Chair of Global Studies.

DUFFY. Congratulations.

*

ANA *returns home to find her mother sitting morosely in the dim light by the telephone.*

ANA. Mum?

BEATRIX. Your brother just phoned.

ANA. David?

BEATRIX. He's just got back to his village.

ANA. You told him?

BEATRIX. Yes.

ANA. Is he coming home?

BEATRIX. No.

Silence.

ANA. Poor David.

Pause.

BEATRIX. Poor George. There'll be hundreds of people at his funeral and the one person he'll be searching for in the crowd won't be there.

POPPY *enters.*

POPPY. I'm sorry. Is this a bad time?

ANA. It is now.

BEATRIX. Ana, please.

ANA. Hey. You expect me to be civil? To this person? (*To* POPPY.) I'm sorry. I don't want you here.

POPPY. Ana. Just hear me out.

ANA. Why?

POPPY. For your father's sake. Lindsay wanted to use George's correspondence to give intellectual prestige to the Institute of Global Studies.

ANA. And I'm supposed to care?

POPPY. Ana, George spent the last two years campaigning against Lindsay and the Institute. It would be such a violation of everything he stood for if we let them use his name and his reputation. I burnt the letters –

ANA. You burnt the letters as an act of revenge.

POPPY. Ana, the letters were not that important to George.

ANA. Oh yeah, right. He would have been happy about you burning them? Is that what you're saying? In fact, he was going to do it himself?

BEATRIX. He can't have cared about them that much, Ana. He left them in Duffy's garage.

ANA. They were packed in archive boxes. (*Pause.*) It's never occurred to you, has it, that I deserved a say in this? That I might've wanted to keep those letters?

POPPY. I'm sorry, Ana. I really wasn't thinking about their value as personal memorabilia.

ANA. I'm sure you weren't.

POPPY. All I thought was that I had to stop Lindsay from using them and making out that she was doing so with his blessing.

ANA. You and Lindsay. You're just the same. You use politics to cover for you. You take the high moral ground, but really you're just being manipulative.

POPPY *is silent.*

POPPY. I'm sorry that's what you think. (*Pause.*) I did want to lash out at her. I admit that. I wanted to rob her of any prestige associated with George, whatsoever. And I had to find a way of asserting my status –

ANA. Status? Is that what you wanted?

POPPY. I just wanted to be acknowledged as George's wife. I thought that was fair enough.

ANA. I'm his daughter. And I've never had any status.

BEATRIX. That's not true.

ANA. Look, I don't think you quite understand. I have spent a large part of my life being ignored by my father. That's

okay. That's just the way it's worked out. But I do have this
need to know who he was. People say you know my father
by reading his books. But I've already done that and I'm
still in the dark. I really hoped that I'd find something in his
private letters . . .

BEATRIX. What is it that you're looking for, Ana?

POPPY. You talk about being ignored by him. That's not how
he saw it. From his point of view he was denied the
opportunity to have a relationship with you.

ANA. What do you mean?

BEATRIX. Are you suggesting that that was my doing?

POPPY. You took his children away.

BEATRIX. And who did he think was going to look after them?
Lindsay? I don't think so. What you don't understand –
because you are such a child of this generation – is that
I gave up my career, I gave up my home, to come here with
him in 1969. So when he decided that he didn't love me
anymore, I wasn't going to give up my children as well.

POPPY. Can I just say this? I didn't fabricate this political
rationalisation. I grew up in a very polite, middle-class
world, thinking that all political activity could be worked
out at the negotiating table. But those bastards are running
roughshod over everyone. They're not being polite, asking
us to the negotiating table. So there comes a time when you
have to act.

ANA. No. There comes a time when you have to organise.
I thought at the very least you would have learnt that from
Dad. Mobilise your supporters. Don't just indulge yourself
in the solitary gesture.

BEATRIX. I think it was an act of radicalism, worthy of
George. And by that I mean – impulsive, passionate and full
of folly. But then I'm a polite, middle-class conservative.

*

DUFFY *and* LINDSAY *are at Duffy's house.*

LINDSAY. Do I have to tell them? Beatrix and Ana?

DUFFY. That's up to you.

LINDSAY. I'm not telling her.

DUFFY. Poppy? She already knows.

LINDSAY. What?

DUFFY. I told her this morning.

LINDSAY. Duffy!

DUFFY. The fact that George had this daughter is not something you can keep to yourself anymore.

LINDSAY. Why not?

DUFFY. Because I won't let you. I've known you for twenty years, Lin, and I know that one of your great skills is 'managing the flow of information'. It's a little strategy –

LINDSAY. That's not –

DUFFY. Sssh. It's a little strategy that's made you very powerful. But this is not information –

LINDSAY. Duffy –

DUFFY. – and I want you to hear this – this is not information which you have control over, anymore. I'm sorry, but I'm not going to stand by and let Poppy drive herself insane, thinking that the man she loved died in the arms of another woman.

*

The following morning BEATRIX *and* ANA *are having breakfast.* ANA *offers her mother a croissant.*

BEATRIX. No croissant for me. I've put on so much weight since I've been here.

ANA. Oh, purlease.

BEATRIX. Look. I can hardly do these pants up.

ANA. Yeah well, I've been meaning to say to you, I think you've really let yourself go. Can you pass the butter please?

She takes a huge glob and puts it ostentatiously on her croissant. BEATRIX *picks it off, just as swiftly.*

BEATRIX. Stop it.

There is a knock at the door. LINDSAY *arrives. When* BEATRIX *opens the door, she finds* LINDSAY *wearing dark glasses.*

Lindsay! You look shocking.

ANA (*to the audience*). As the first wife said to the second wife.

LINDSAY. I haven't slept since 1959. Have you got some strong coffee?

ANA. Croissant?

LINDSAY. Ugh, no thanks.

BEATRIX. Lindsay, I think there are some things we need to talk through. We had Poppy here last night.

LINDSAY. So you know then.

BEATRIX. Know what?

LINDSAY. About . . . Rachel.

ANA. Who's Rachel?

LINDSAY. Poppy didn't tell you?

BEATRIX. No.

LINDSAY. I'm surprised. She must have a modicum of integrity. (*Pause.*) Rachel Doyle – the girl in the plane – was my daughter. I'm sorry to tell you. I . . . relinquished her for adoption, a couple of days after she was born.

BEATRIX. You had a daughter?

LINDSAY. George never knew. Until about six months ago. (*Pause.*) I never told him.

ANA. I'm sorry. I don't understand. George was the father?

LINDSAY. Yes.

ANA. You didn't tell him?

LINDSAY. No.

ANA. But how come he didn't know you were pregnant?

LINDSAY. I went to Sydney. It was a long time ago.

BEATRIX. So. This girl. How old is she?

LINDSAY. Twenty-eight.

ANA. Same age as me.

LINDSAY (*nodding*). I'm sorry.

BEATRIX. Are you sure this isn't information that you should have told me alone?

LINDSAY. I didn't want to tell either of you, Bea. I never have. But now this has happened, I thought Ana should hear it from me.

BEATRIX. And you've never met her, this girl?

LINDSAY. No.

BEATRIX. You've never met your daughter?

LINDSAY. No.

BEATRIX. I'm sorry, Lindsay. I'm truly sorry.

The lights fade.

*

We hear the sound of a plane roaring overhead. When the lights come up, ANA *is at the Island. She is on a swing.*

ANA. So. Dad, I have a sister. What a balls-up. Just as well you didn't know about it all that time. One more example of the women in your life taking care of business. I appreciate that, under the circumstances, this may sound petty – but I would just like to remind you of all the times you and

Lindsay and Mum mocked me for being so prim. So uptight. 'Ana is such a blue-stocking.' 'It's her generation. They're all like that. Prudish!'

Do you remember when I knitted you that pair of purple socks for Christmas? Probably not. The first time I saw you wearing those socks was up there in the sand dunes. You were having sex with that poetess, Fredrica someone? I was playing on the beach when I saw my socks – up there – on the end of a pair of feet. When I crept closer, there you were. Fornicating with a South American. Honestly . . .

So, with hindsight, given the complete cock-up you've made of your personal life, you would have to concede that your astonishing profligacy is not exactly the perfect blueprint for how one should live one's life.

(*To the audience.*) I haven't been to the Island for years. When I was little, we used to play beach cricket here at dusk. This is Collie Beach. The two families – Duffy and his lot, and us, with different hangers-on. All these people used to come down from Melbourne and Sydney, to stay at the house in summer. Dad never wore any clothes on the beach. He didn't give a damn. It was really humiliating. I refused to invite any of my friends. No way. It wasn't like he had a great body or anything –

A shaggy, wet tennis ball flies onto the stage. ANA *catches it.* GEORGE'S GHOST *appears, wielding an old cricket bat.* ANA *stares.*

At least you're not in the nuddy. That's a relief.

GEORGE. I think weight-for-height, and considering my age, I'm in pretty good nick.

ANA. You're dead, for Chris'sake.

GEORGE. Yes, there is that.

ANA. The police said that she was flying the plane. Rachel.

GEORGE. Yes, she was.

ANA. You handed over the controls.

GEORGE. Yes. You're not really flying otherwise.

ANA. Do you think she 'reached out her hand and touched the face of God'?

GEORGE. I hope so.

ANA. Why didn't you take me flying? (*Pause.*) I lack the imagination?

GEORGE *shakes his head.*

But I was never really clever enough, was I? Or beautiful? Or slim?

GEORGE. Rachel worked in a cake shop in Wangaratta. She wasn't exactly svelte.

ANA. The fact that you actually cared about a big, fat girl from the country makes me think more highly of you. (*Pause.*) Did I ever tell you about the time – a couple of years ago – I was in this bookstore in Fitzroy? There was this guy there – I'd met him at a party the night before. He was sitting cross-legged on the floor reading one of your books. I said, 'What are you reading that crap for?' And he said, 'Moral courage'. He was reading your book for moral courage. At the time I thought he was a dipstick. You wanted me to adopt your whole political and moral value system, didn't you?

GEORGE. Yes, I did.

ANA. Why would I want to do that? When it didn't extend to taking proper care of the people you love and who loved you. I'm trying to forgive you for creating a mess.

GEORGE. You can't have a feast without creating a mess.

ANA. You're unrepentant.

GEORGE. I'm dead.

Pause.

ANA. Dad, I don't think I know what moral courage actually is.

GEORGE. Of course you do.

ANA. Was it an act of moral courage to burn your letters?

GEORGE. I think it would be an act of moral courage to make it stand for something. (*Beat.*) Every day, people like Lindsay are justifying their compromises. They say, 'In principle I agree, but the reality is I have no choice'. But you do have a choice.

ANA. You had choices all along about your family.

GEORGE. I wrote to the future in a lot of different ways, Ana. But ultimately the great leap of faith, the great expression of hopefulness – is to have a child. If I've had one fundamental belief, it's about the power of hopefulness. I think hope is a moral responsibility.

ANA. I think it's a personality trait.

GEORGE. You have to understand that idealism is not the same as naiveté. When I talk about idealism I'm talking about the capacity to imagine a better future. That was my life's work.

ANA. If you mean what you say, that there are many paths to the future, you have to let me find my own. (*Pause.*) But I want your blessing.

GEORGE *kisses* ANA. *He pushes the swing. He exits.*

*

Funeral music. The coffin is carried on and placed centre stage. DUFFY *moves to the podium and addresses the audience.*

DUFFY. Ladies and gentlemen. Welcome. I'm Alan Duffy and I want to thank you for coming today to mourn the passing of our friend and colleague, Peter George. And to celebrate his extraordinary life. We are joined today by the three remarkable women in George's life. Beatrix George, his first wife.

Focus on BEATRIX.

Mother of his children, Ana and David.

Focus on LINDSAY.

Professor Lindsay Graham, George's second wife.

Focus on POPPY.

His third wife, Poppy Santini, who has been at his side for the past two years . . .

ANA *enters the church.*

. . . and his daughter. Ladies and gentleman – Ana George.

ANA *moves to the lectern.*

ANA (*to the audience*). My father taught us to marvel at the power of ideas. But he was committed to the principle that ideas and knowledge belonged to everyone. To all of us. To honour humanity. In everything he wrote there is one recurring truth: that the people have the capacity to be the authors of their own history and their own destiny. I loved him. We all loved him. And he knew what it meant to love each of us: my mother Beatrix, my brother David, Lindsay, Poppy, Duffy and Rachel. But we can no longer be defined by being his wives, his children or his friends. Nor do we find definition by endless self-scrutiny. That way lies the very loneliness that defines our age; the very selfish individualism which George fought to expose. We are defined by our shared humanity. And we are inspired by the qualities which Peter George embodied – hopefulness and moral courage. This is my first letter to the future.

ANA *plays a piece of music she has composed.*

The End.